MW01670722

How to Beat a DUI

James Nesci

Lawyers & Judges Publishing Company, Inc.

This publication is designed to provide accurate and authoritative information in regard to the subject matter covered. It is sold with the understanding that the publisher is not engaged in rendering legal, accounting, or other professional service. If legal advice or other expert assistance is required, the services of a competent professional person should be sought.

—From a Declaration of Principles jointly adopted by
Committee of the American Bar Association
and a Committee of Publishers and Associations.

The publisher, editors and authors must disclaim any liability, in whole or in part, arising from the information in this volume. The reader is urged to verify the reference material prior to any detrimental reliance thereupon. Since this material deals with legal, medical and engineering information, the reader is urged to consult with an appropriate licensed professional prior to taking any action that might involve any interpretation or application of information within the realm of a licensed professional practice.

Copyright ©2008 by Authentic Anatomical, a division of Lawyers & Judges Publishing. All rights reserved. All chapters are the product of the Authors and do not reflect the opinions of the Publisher, or of any other person, entity, or company. No part of this book may be reproduced in any form or by any means, including photocopy, or electronic use, without permission from the Publisher's representative at the Copyright Clearance Center, Inc. (CCC) at www.copyright.com.

AUTHENTIC ANATOMICAL

A Division of Lawyers & Judges Publishing
P.O. Box 30040 • Tucson, AZ 85751-0040
(800) 209-7109 • FAX (800) 330-8795
e-mail: sales@lawyersandjudges.com
www.lawyersandjudges.com

Library of Congress Cataloging-in-Publication Data

Nesci, James.
How to beat a DUI / James Nesci.
p. cm.
Includes index.
ISBN-13: 978-1-933264-48-6 (softcover : alk. paper)
ISBN-10: 1-933264-48-9 (softcover : alk. paper)
1. Drunk driving--United States. 2. Defense (Criminal procedure)--United States. I. Title.
KF2231.N47 2008
345.73'0247--dc22

2008003407

ISBN 13: 978-1-933264-48-6
ISBN 10: 1-933264-48-9
Printed in the United States of America
10 9 8 7 6 5 4 3 2 1

To my wife and kids for always supporting me throughout this and other projects.

To my partners, Joseph P. St. Louis and Steven D. West, for allowing me the time to write this book.

And special thanks to Wayne R. Foote, who took time out from his busy law practice in Bangor, Maine, to do a substantive edit on this book.

Contents

Glossary of DUI Terms

This glossary contains some of the most common terms as used in DUI cases and investigations. Many of the terms have common meanings outside of the DUI area as well. Italicized terms used in the definitions are found elsewhere in the glossary.

Absorptive Phase: That portion of the disposition of alcohol in human beings where alcohol is being absorbed into the blood stream from the stomach and intestines. Contrast with *Elimination Phase.*

Acetone: A volatile chemical found on the breath of some people (usually diabetics), under certain circumstances. It can be mistaken for ethyl alcohol by some infrared breath testers.

Acquittal: A Not Guilty verdict or a dismissal with prejudice.

Actual Physical Control: Operating controls of a vehicle without actually driving the vehicle (i.e. being parked, engine on, and sitting in the driver's seat may be considered Actual Physical Control in some jurisdictions). See also: *Physical Control.*

Affirmative Defense: A defense at trial where the burden of producing evidence falls on the defendant, rather than on the prosecution. It is most commonly seen as a *Rising BAC Defense*. It has been eliminated in some states.

Aggravated DUI: The term differs from state-to-state. In some states, "aggravated" means "felony," and in other states, it simply means that the DUI is punishable by a higher mandatory minimum sentence than a non-aggravated DUI offense.

Aliquat (Blood Testing): The defined portion of the blood sample used for testing purposes.

Alveolar Air: Air which comes from the alveolar sacs at the deepest part of the lungs. Despite the common regulatory requirement of alveolar air, it is impossible to obtain a pure-alveolar air sample without killing the subject. It is often thought of as deep-lung air.

Anti-Coagulant (Blood Testing): Found within the *Grey-top Blood Tubes*, the anti-coagulant keeps the blood in liquid form. It is usually Potassium Oxalate or EDTA.

Appeal: A review by a higher court of a legal decision. The government may not appeal a Not Guilty verdict.

Appellant: The party who brings the *Appeal* (i.e. the party that lost in the lower court).

Appellee: The party against whom the *Appeal* is taken (i.e. the party that won in the lower court).

Autosampler (Blood Testing): A mechanical device, usually a carousel, used to automatically place *Headspace Vials* in the proper order for blood testing.

Blood Alcohol Content (BAC): The amount of alcohol in human blood defined as a percentage. Also a blood test result, usually expressed in terms of grams of alcohol per 100 milliliters of blood.

Blood Kit (Blood Testing): A box which (usually) contains everything necessary for a forensic blood draw. The kit will contain antiseptic swabs, two grey-top blood tubes and seals for the kit. Some kits also contain a syringe, hub, and a urine-collection container.

Blood Split (Blood Testing): A second sample or tube of blood used for defense-testing purposes (not an *Independent Sample*).

Breath Alcohol Content (BrAC)(Breath Testing): Breath test results expressed as grams of alcohol per 210 liters of breath.

Calibrator (Blood Testing): An aqueous solution of a known alcohol concentration which is used to set a benchmark for a headspace gas chromatograph to compare against blood samples of unknown concentration.

Candida Albicans (Blood Testing): Yeast. When introduced into a blood sample, the yeast can consume sugars in the blood and produce ethyl alcohol in the blood tube.

Case Law: Rule of law set down by case decisions, as opposed to *Statutes*.

Chromatogram (Blood Testing): A graphical representation of the volatiles in a *Headspace Gas Chromatography* sample.

Criminalist: Same as *Forensic Toxicologist*.

Column (Blood Testing): A very thin tube used in *Headspace Gas Chromatography* to separate volatile substances from each other by both mechanical and chemical means. Columns may be "packed columns" loaded with crushed fire brick or diatomaceous earth, or more commonly are "capillary columns" lined with a proprietary substance.

Complaint: Formal notice of charges, usually presented by way of a traffic ticket.

Control (Blood Testing): A blood sample of a known value run alongside unknown samples as a check on the system.

Defendant: One who stands accused of a crime.

Deficient Sample (Breath Testing): A breath sample where a minimum volume of air is not met. Required volumes of air differ depending on which brand and model of breath testing device is used. Also known as an "insufficient sample".

Deprivation Period (Breath Testing): A defined period of time in which a breath test subject is not allowed to eat, smoke or drink anything. Nothing is to enter or leave the mouth. Less-strict than an *Observation Period*.

Divided Attention Task: An exercise which requires the subject to complete both a physical and mental task at the same time. The inability of the subject to divide his attention between the physical and mental tasks may be a sign of impairment.

Drug Evaluation Classification Procedure (DECP): Also known as a Drug Recognition Evaluation, it is a 12-step process in which a qualified police investigator uses deductive and inductive reasoning, speculation and guess-work to conclude that the subject has ingested one or more of seven classes of drugs. Most often, the conclusion of the officer, but not necessarily the observations of this officer, matches the drug that the subject admitted to using prior to the DECP.

Drug Recognition Evaluator (DRE): One who is qualified under NHTSA and IACP guidelines to administer a Drug Recognition Evaluation. Also known as "DRT," Drug Recognition Technician.

Dry-Gas Standard: A pressurized canister of ethanol and nitrogen used to check calibration of a breath tester (See *Simulator*).

DUI: Driving Under the Influence. **DWI:** Driving While Impaired. **DWAI:** Driving While Ability is Impaired. **DWUI:** Driving While Under the Influence. **OWI:** Operating While Intoxicated

Elimination Phase: The portion of the disposition of alcohol in a human being where alcohol is being eliminated from the body and absorption is complete. Contrast with *Absorptive Phase*.

Equilibrium: A state of balance between opposing forces, whether they be static or dynamic.

Ethyl Alcohol (EtOH): Alcohol found in beverages.

Evidential Breath Testing Device (EBT): A breath tester that produces results admissible in court under certain circumstances. See *Preliminary Breath Test.*

Evidentiary Hearing (EH): A courtroom hearing where evidence is admitted and testimony taken. It is used as a forum to determine the outcome of pretrial motions.

Expungement: The erasure of a criminal record.

Field Sobriety Test (FST): A physical test used by the police to determine whether there is enough *Probable Cause* to arrest a suspect. (See also: *Standardized Field Sobriety Test*).

Forensic Toxicologist: A scientist who is called upon to analyze poisons, breath test evidence, and bodily fluids and to testify in the form of a scientific opinion in court regarding such analysis.

Grand Jury: A group of citizens chosen to determine whether charges should be filed against an individual.

Grey-Top Tube: The blood tube of choice for DUI investigations. Originally designed and used for glucose determinations, the grey-top tube has a *Preservative* and *Anti-coagulant* in it.

Headspace Gas Chromatography (Blood Testing): An indirect method of determining blood alcohol concentration by separating volatile components in the blood and quantifying their amounts.

Headspace Vial (Blood Testing): A sealed container used to hold an *Aliquat* of blood for headspace testing.

Ignition Interlock Devices (IID): A breath testing device installed on a vehicle which requires the driver to blow into it prior to starting the vehicle. Most IID's require the driver to periodically retest after the vehicle has been started. Generally, if the driver's recorded breath alcohol concentration is below .003, the vehicle will start. Some IID's are set to a .000 tolerance.

Horizontal Gaze Nystagmus (HGN): A type of field sobriety test in which the eyes are examined. It is an involuntary jerking of the eyes along a horizontal plane. All humans have HGN, but alcohol and some drugs classes make it more pronounced. It is loosely and unscientifically correlated to different *Blood Alcohol Concentrations*, the levels of which vary from study to study.

Implied Consent: By simply driving, the driver has agreed to be tested for alcohol content or drugs by chemical means (breath, blood, urine or other bodily substance). Typically, those people who are incapable of expressly agreeing to a chemical test (i.e. dead or unconscious) are deemed not to have withdrawn their consent to be tested.

Independent Sample (Blood Testing): Most commonly a sample of blood drawn by the suspect's chosen phlebotomist and facility and analyzed at the suspect's designated lab. This is distinguished from a *Blood Split*.

Indictment: Formal filing of charges, usually by *Grand Jury*.

Infrared Spectroscopy (Breath Testing): The most common method of analyzing breath for alcohol content. It is achieved by shining infrared light at a detector and measuring the quantity of light that strikes the detector to set a baseline. A sample is then introduced into the chamber and the reduction in infrared light which strikes the detector is measured and calculated via a mathematical formula to determine *Breath Alcohol Concentration.*

Internal Standard (Blood Testing): A volatile substance of known amount mixed into a blood sample and used for comparative purposes to measure the amount of alcohol in a given sample.

International Association of Chiefs of Police (IACP): A police organization which creates non binding policies for police agencies and published police manuals and recommends certain police protocols such as *SFST* Guidelines.

Miranda Rights: A set of warnings that a suspect, who is in custody, must be advised of before the police can ask questions about the crime that is being investigated. Miranda Rights are as follows:

> You have the right to remain silent.
> Anything you say can, and will, be used against you in a court of law.
> You have the right to have an attorney present with you prior to and during questioning if you so desire.
> If you cannot afford an attorney, one will be appointed to you.
> Do you understand your rights?

Motion in Limine: Literally "at the door." A legal question to be determined immediately before a trial begins. Generally Motions in Limine are of a legal nature, not an evidentiary nature.

Mouth Alcohol (Breath Testing): Alcohol that is contained in the mouth, as opposed to the lungs. If the *Evidential Breath Tester* does not recognize mouth alcohol and alert the operator, it will result in a falsely elevated result.

Mouth Piece (Breath Testing): A small, plastic disposable device used at the end of a breath tester's breath hose. Mouth pieces must be changed for every breath sample.

National Highway Traffic Safety Administration (NHTSA): A federal regulatory agency charged with keeping the roadways safe. A small, but very publicized portion of NHTSA is their Impaired Driving Division which provides support to police organizations in their anti-drunk driving efforts. NHTSA also funds impaired-driving studies and provides police agencies with manuals regarding every aspect of a DUI investigation.

National Institute of Standards and Technology (NIST): A non-regulatory federal agency that defines weights and measures for testing and comparison purposes. Their stated mission is to develop and promote measurement, standards, and technology to enhance productivity, facilitate trade, and improve the quality of life.

Observation Period (Breath Testing): A continuous period of time during which a breath test subject is observed prior to submitting to a breath test. During this time period, the subject may not burp, vomit, belch, ingest anything or remove anything from the mouth.

One-Leg-Stand (OLS): A field sobriety test task that is both validated and standardized by the National Highway Traffic Safety Administration. The test requires the subject to balance on one leg for approximately 30 seconds. There are four possible cues on the test. It is a divided attention task.

Passive Alcohol Sensor (Breath Testing): A breath alcohol tester that tests ambient air by simply being placed near the subject's face.

Per Se: Latin for "on the face of it." Per se laws make one strictly liable for driving with a prohibited alcohol concentration. No criminal intent is necessary.

Physical Control: Operating controls of a vehicle without actually driving the vehicle (i.e. being parked, engine on, and sitting in the driver's seat may be considered Physical Control in some jurisdictions). See also: *Actual Physical Control.*

Pipette (Blood Testing): A laboratory device used to dispense liquids in precise amounts. Generally, it works on the same principle as an eye-dropper.

Plasma (Blood Testing): A liquid portion made from whole blood by centrifuging the sample until it separates. Plasma includes fibrinogen, which is a clotting agent. Alcohol testing of plasma can yield results up to 18% or more higher than whole blood. See *Serum.*

Plea: A criminal defendant's initial answer to an indictment of complaint. There are only three pleas relevant to a DUI: Guilty, Not Guilty and No Contest.

Plea Bargain: A contract between a prosecuting agency and a criminal defendant where the defendant pleads guilty or no contest to the stated charges, amended charges or reduced charges in return for a lesser sentence or some other benefit.

Povidone Iodine (Blood Testing): A non-alcohol based antiseptic used to cleanse the suspect's arm before a blood draw.

Precedent: *Case Law* which sets down a rule of law to be followed by lower courts.

Prejudice: A designation for dismissal of charges. If a charge is dismissed without prejudice, the prosecuting agency may refile the charge within a defined time-period. If a charge is dismissed with prejudice, the prosecuting agency must appeal to a higher court before being able to refile the charge. A not guilty verdict has the effect of dismissal with prejudice, but the prosecuting agency is barred from an appeal.

Preliminary Alcohol Screening (PAS)(Breath Testing): A breath test taken before an evidential breath test. Admissibility of a PAS is uncommon in most states, but not all states. California is a notable exception. Same as *Preliminary Breath Test (PBT).*

Preliminary Breath Test (PBT)(Breath Testing): A breath test taken before an evidential breath test. Admissibility of a PBT is uncommon in most states, but not all states. California is a notable exception. Same as *Preliminary Alcohol Screening (PAS).*

Preservative (Blood Testing): An anti-glycolytic agent (usually sodium flouride) found in *Grey-top Tubes* which prevents glycolosis of the sample.

Probable Cause (Legal Standard): A level of proof necessary to arrest a person.

Prosecutor: The government's lawyer charged with the duty of prosecuting criminal cases.

Quality Assurance Specialist (QAS)(Breath Testing): A person who maintains breath testing equipment.

Radio Frequency Interference (RFI)(Breath Testing): A type of electromagnetic wave that can alter a breath test result. Most modern infrared evidential breath testers have a radio frequency interference antenna, RFI shielding and software that is programmed to alert the operator to RFI and abort the test. These three safeguards do not always work.

Reasonable Suspicion (Legal Standard): A level of proof necessary to detain a person for investigative purposes (less than *Probable Cause*).

Recantation of Refusal: A person who is required to submit to a chemical test may refuse to submit, then change his or her mind and ultimately submit to the test. Recantation is subject to specific circumstances and rules and may be prohibited altogether in some jurisdictions.

Refusal: A person who is required to submit to a chemical test may refuse to submit. Refusal may have severe consequences or no consequences, depending upon the jurisdiction.

Replicate Breath Test (Breath Testing): Two breath samples, taken within specific time limits, that must agree with each other by a specific margin, and immediately preceded by a deprivation or observation period.

Retrograde Extrapolation: A mathematical formula for determining what a person's alcohol concentration was at an earlier point in time, based on a known alcohol concentration at a later point in time. A retrograde extrapolation requires that the person be in the *Elimination Phase* and assumes an elimination rate. Retrograde extrapolation is often highly speculative and open to attack.

Rising BAC Defense: A legal defense where the driver may have been over the per se limit at the time of the chemical test, but was under the limit at the time of driving because all of the alcohol had not yet been absorbed into the bloodstream. This defense is not available is some states. See *Absorptive Phase* and *Affirmative Defense*.

Serum (Blood Testing): Whole blood minus the clotting element (fibrinogen). It is created from whole blood by allowing the blood to stand and separate on its own. Alcohol testing of serum can yield results 18% or more higher than whole blood. See *Plasma*.

Simulator: Also known as a wet-bath simulator, it is a device where a solution of alcohol and water is used to create a headspace-gas alcohol concentration to be introduced into a breath tester to check calibration (See *Dry-Gas Standard*).

Slope Detector (Breath Testing): A computer program within a breath testing device that is used to detect *Mouth Alcohol*, alert the operator and abort the test.

Standardized Field Sobriety Test (SFST): A physical test used by the police to determine whether there is enough *Probable Cause* to arrest a suspect. An SFST is a sub-category of *Field Sobriety Tests* and has been *Validated* and standardized. "Standardized" simply means that the test is done in the same manner and evaluated using the same criteria each and every time the test is administered. Thus, an officer in New York will give the exact same test as an officer in California and evaluate the results in the same manner. There are only three SFSTs which have been standardized and validated. They are the *Horizontal Gaze Nystagmus (HGN)*, *Walk-and-Turn (WAT)* and *One-Leg-Stand (OLS)*.

Statute: Law created by a legislative body as opposed to *Case Law*.

Summons: A court order directing a person to appear at a specific time and location to answer an *Indictment* or *Complaint*.

Validated: It denotes a *Standardized Field Sobriety Test* which has been correlated to a particular alcohol concentration within the subject being tested. Do not confuse the term "validated" with "valid" as the latter term has a connotation of truth and accuracy.

Vertical Gaze Nystagmus (VGN): A type of field sobriety test in which the eyes are examined. It is an involuntary jerking of the eyes along a vertical plane. It is used as part of the *Drug Evaluation Classification Protocol* and is not correlated to any *Blood Alcohol Concentration.*

Voir Dire: Initial questioning of the jury panel to determine fitness to serve as a juror.

Walk-and-Turn (WAT): A field sobriety test task that is both validated and standardized by the National Highway Traffic Safety Administration. The test requires the subject to walk nine heel-to-toe steps down a line, turn and walk nine steps back in the same fashion. There are eight possible cues on the test.It is a divided attention task.

White's Retrograde Extrapolation: A mathematical formula for determining how many drinks must be left unabsorbed in a person's stomach for that person to have been under the per se limit at the time of driving. (See *Retrograde Extrapolation*).

Whole Blood (Blood Testing): That portion of the blood which has been drawn and is used for forensic testing purposes. Whole blood has not be altered in any way to remove any components of the blood sample, although *Preservatives* and *Anti-coagulants* may have been added.

Widmark's Formula: A mathematical equation which is used to calculate an approximate alcohol concentration in a human being. It requires knowledge of the subject's body weight, gender, type of alcoholic drink, and phase of alcohol consumption.

Foreword

What This Book Is

Whether it is called DUI, DWI, DWAI, or OUI, it is the only criminal offense that touches the non-criminal's life. Although DUI is not a political crime, it is a highly politicized crime. We have moved away from the original intent of DUI laws, which were to remove those people who are a hazard to others on the roadway. Now, we simply prosecute people based on junk science and innuendo. DUI is a serious charge that can leave you with a permanent criminal record. DUI is a charge worth fighting.

This book is a guide to help people understand what DUI is and how to help your attorney defend you. This book is meant to foster a dialogue between you and your attorney. Most people visit an attorney after a DUI arrest and have no idea of what questions to ask or what information may be important to their cases. Sometimes the attorney will fail to fully explore the DUI case. This book should help the attorney cover all of the issues. Education is your best defense against a DUI charge.

What this Book Is Not

This book is not a license to drive drunk. People who drive drunk can hurt or kill themselves and others. Never take the risk. If you feel that you have had too much to drink to drive safely, don't drive. Take a cab. Take a bus. Have a sober friend drive you home. Walk home. Don't risk your life and liberty or the lives of others. Prisons are full of people who wish that they could take back that decision to drive. Don't add to that population.

This book is not a substitute for your attorney's advice. Hopefully you picked your attorney because you trust his or her judgment. Jurisdictional issues are specific to the jurisdiction and, sometimes, to the individual courthouse. In writing this book, I cannot anticipate all local rules and policies. The bottom line is: Trust your attorney.

The Truth About DUI

Police, prosecutors and Mothers Against Drunk Driving (MADD) want the public to believe that the majority of drunk drivers kill people. This is simply not true.

Benjamin Disraeli said, "There are three kinds of lies: lies, damned lies and statistics." This quote is never more relevant than when one examines the manner in which government traffic death statistics are twisted and tortured in order to press for an agenda of prohibition.

MADD often touts figures for the number of drunk driving deaths each year in the United States. In 2004, MADD claims nearly 16,694 drunk driving deaths occurred. But what does this figure actually represent?

In 2004, there were 42,636 "Traffic Fatalities" according to the National Center for Statistics and Analysis (NCSA). That's almost 117 people killed in traffic accidents every day in the 50 states, Washington, D.C. and Puerto Rico. California had the most with 4,120 deaths and Washington, D.C. had the least with 43. The NCSA Fatality Analysis Reporting System (FARS) classifies nearly 40% of the total number of traffic deaths as "Alcohol Related Traffic Fatalities." But the question arises: Are they actually related to alcohol, or was alcohol simply present, in some amount, in one or more people at the accident scene?

Alcohol Related Traffic Fatalities would include a drunk driver who rear-ends and kills a sober motorcyclist waiting at a traffic light. It would also include the reverse: a sober driver who rear-ends and kills a drunken motorcyclist sitting at the same traffic light. Clearly the drunken motorcyclist was not at fault, but the death would be reported as an Alcohol Related Traffic Fatality. This, in turn, is presented to the public as a drunk driving death.

It is important to realize that Alcohol Related Traffic Fatalities include those people with known Blood Alcohol Concentrations and estimated Blood Alcohol Concentrations. In fact, more than half of the Alcohol Related Traffic Fatalities had estimated Blood Alcohol Concentrations. Generally, the estimate is left up to the discretion of local police.

DUI is big business. Governmental agencies dole out cash to police agencies like candy. And the police agencies are all too eager to jump on the bandwagon to receive such goodies as new patrol cars, police equipment and special monetary incentives for overtime and special operations. Most DUI arrests are made at night. Most courts hold proceedings during the day. Police who work special DUI squads get extra pay for nighttime shifts, special shifts and overtime during the day. Working a DUI detail is a prime position for most police officers. States receive millions of dollars in federal highway funds for compliance with arbitrary DUI laws. Courts receive special attention for so-called "DUI Offender Programs" which encourage people to plead guilty. Crime labs, courts, prosecuting agencies, police departments and government agencies receive funds from people convicted of DUI.

Those who stand between the government and the accused citizen, often for little pay and even less glory, are DUI defense attorneys. There is no other area of criminal law as complex or challenging. Those of us who do what we do are not in it for the money. We are in it because we believe that every time another bogus anti-drunk driving law is passed, a little piece of the Constitution dies.

About the Author

James Nesci is a 1994 graduate of the University of Arizona College of Law and was a solo practitioner for ten years in Tucson, Arizona, before becoming the managing partner in the firm Nesci, St. Louis & West, P.L.L.C. in January 2005.

In 1999 Mr. Nesci became a Sustaining Member of the National College for DUI Defense. In 2001, he was Board Certified by the National College for DUI Defense, Inc. and is one of only two Board Certified attorneys in the State of Arizona and one of only thirty-four in the nation (as of April 2008). In 2006, he was appointed Regent of the National College for DUI Defense, Inc. He currently serves as the chair of the Curriculum Committee for the NCDD.

He is the author of *Arizona DUI Defense: The Law and Practice*, a legal treatise written for DUI defense attorneys and published by Lawyers & Judges Publishing Company. He has written the Defense Chapter for the Fifth Edition of the treatise: *Medicolegal Aspects of Alcohol*, which is a text used by forensic toxicologists across the world and serves as the text for the Borkenstein School at Indiana University.

His firm's practice is devoted entirely to criminal defense. At any one time, he typically defends about fifteen DUI cases in several jurisdictions while other members of the firm defend DUI, capital murder, rape, armed robbery, possession and varied federal cases. Both of his partners are death-penalty qualified.

Mr. Nesci often defends cases well into the .30 blood-alcohol range. He has caught more than one police officer lying during cross-examination and some police officers have even refused to grant pretrial interviews to him without a prosecutor or their own counsel present. He was one of the lead attorneys on the Intoximeters® RBT-IV breath-testing issue in Southern Arizona which resulted in the suppression of breath tests in over 3,000 cases and the removal of the RBT-IV from the streets of Arizona. He represented former Supremes lead singer Diana Ross and Tampa Bay Buccaneers' Tight-End Jerramy Stevens on Extreme DUI charges.

Mr. Nesci is a team-player within the Southern Arizona DUI Defense Community. He is often involved in large-scale challenges to DUI investigative methods and chemical testing. His opinion is sought by DUI Attorneys across the nation on various issues. He is one of only a handful of attorneys in the country who holds a DOT-Compliant Permit to operate an Intoxilyzer® 8000. He owns both an Intoxilyzer® 5000 and 8000 which are used for in-court demonstrations and for research purposes. He is qualified to administer Standardized Field Sobriety Tests under National Highway Traffic Safety Administration and International Association of Chiefs of Police Guidelines.

Mr. Nesci has lectured from coast-to-coast for such organizations as The University of Arizona James E. Rogers College of Law, Arizona State University College of Law CLE Department, the University of Mississippi CLE Department, South Texas College of Law CLE Department, Arizona Attorneys for Criminal Justice, Arizona Public Defenders Association, California Attorneys for Criminal Justice, Florida Association of Criminal Defense Lawyers, National Association of Criminal Defense Lawyers, the National College for DUI Defense, the Nevada State Bar Association, New York State Bar Association, Texas Criminal Defense Lawyers Association, the Ohio Association of Criminal Defense Lawyers, Maryland Criminal Defense Attorneys Association, the Louisiana Association of Criminal Defense Lawyers, Mexican-American Bar Association at Loyola, Washington Foundation for Criminal Justice, City of Phoenix and Maricopa County Public Defender's Offices, Maricopa County Bar Association, and the Pima County Bar Association.

He has taught seminars on the subjects of Fourth Amendment Law, Drug Recognition Evaluations (DUI-Drugs), Cross-Examination, Trial Tactics, Jury Selection, Field Sobriety Testing, Blood Alcohol Calculations, Opening and Closing Arguments, Ethics, Frye and Daubert Challenges, Intoxilyzer 8000 Operator's Course, Headspace Gas Chromatography, Blood and Breath Testing. He is a frequent guest of the John C. Scott radio program in Tucson. The Tucson Weekly named Mr. Nesci "King of the DUI Defense" (December 19, 2002). He has appeared on CNN, Inside Edition, Celebrity Justice, Fox News, Access Hollywood and Court TV.

Chapter 1

DUI Laws

Synopsis

1.1 Chapter Overview

DUI laws can be divided into several categories. This chapter looks at the differences between the law and the elements of proof required for each. Keep in mind that DUI laws vary from state-to-state with significant differences. Defenses also vary from state-to-state.

1.2 DUI Impairment Laws

A. Driver vs. Driving

Every state has DUI laws based on some sort of impairment. This is the original drunk driving offense. The relevant question used to be: Did you have too much to drink to be able to drive safely? However, it is no longer that simple.

Most states have moved away from the simple question to more complex issues that focus not on the driving behavior, but on the driver. The relevant question might range from whether the *driving* was materially and appreciably affected by the alcohol consumed to whether the *driver* was impaired to the slightest degree by the alcohol consumed. To this end, Field Sobriety Testing becomes one of the government's most important pieces of evidence. Take, for example, the case where the police have seen no bad driving, but instead have made a stop based on an equipment violation such as a license-plate light being burned out, or for an expired registration tag.

Since there is no bad driving, those people accused under laws which focus on driving more than the driver will stand a better chance of winning at trial However, one can be impaired, yet have a fact pattern with no bad driving. In states where the focus is on the driver, the FSTs and observations of the officer become more relevant.

In states where the focus is on the driving, the FSTs and observations of the officers are far less relevant. When someone is charged with DUI and a civil traffic violation of weaving, chances are significantly worse of winning because the prosecution can point to bad driving as evidence of the offense and need not provide evidence of FSTs to the jury.

Good driving is always a defense to DUI, but clearly it is better to be in a jurisdiction where the focus is on the driving, not on the driver.

Generally, elements that the prosecution must prove are: Driving (or physical control of the vehicle) and Impairment due to alcohol or drugs or any combination of the two.

1.3 Per Se Laws

Per Se Laws are laws which prohibit driving with a specified blood alcohol concentration (BAC) or with any class of named drugs in your system, irrespective of their effect upon the driver. Originally, a chemical test (breath, blood or urine) was introduced as relevant evidence in the traditional impairment-based DUI offense. No one from either the defense or the prosecution would ever argue that BAC is irrelevant to whether a person is impaired by alcohol or not. The argument lies in the amount. There are some studies which show impairment for certain activities with as little as .02 BAC and some which show no impairment for some activities as high as .20. The recent trend in scientific studies, however, is to show impairment as low as possible. This is a function of the process for funding the studies. For example, if one were to propose a study to the National Highway Traffic Safety Administration (NHTSA) to show that no one is impaired for the task of driving until they reach a .20 BAC, and ask for only $50,000 to fund it, NHTSA would reject it out-of-hand because they have no interest in providing that information to the public. However, if one were to propose a study which cost ten times as much, seeking to show that everyone is impaired for the task of driving as low as a .02 BAC, NHTSA would rush to fund the study.

Per Se Laws are also tied to highway funding from the federal government. In the 1990s the federal government sought to lower the per se limits for DUI to .08, but since DUI laws are a state matter, they had no legal power to change them. The federal government, however, does hold the purse-strings for highway money. They used this power to force states to change by withholding federal dollars for highway improvement for those states which did not lower their limits. In 2000, twenty-three states had per se BAC laws above .08% and one state even had a per se law at .15. Eight states had no per se laws of any kind. Now, all states have per se laws of .08 and some even have lower limits for DUI-related offenses such as DWAI (Driving While Ability Impaired).

A. Breath, Blood or Urine as a Chemical Test

Breath testing is the most common way to measure the amount of alcohol in a subject. It is both the least invasive type of measurement and the most cost-effective type. It requires minimally trained personnel to accomplish breath testing. And it provides on-the-spot results to both the police and suspect. However, it is subject to huge variables which can render it highly inaccurate. A breath test is never used to detect the presence of drugs.

Blood testing is the most invasive of the tests. Usually, two tubes of blood are drawn and the accused will be allowed access to the second tube for referee testing purposes. Most commonly, headspace gas chromatography will be used. Headspace Gas Chromatography can be a highly accurate measure of BAC, if it is done correctly. However, Headspace GC must be done correctly. As one federal lab inspector said to me: "There are no *Mulligans* in forensic toxicology." You either do it the right way, or the result is completely unreliable. Blood testing can be used to test for alcohol content and the presence of drugs.

Urine is rarely used to determine Blood Alcohol Concentration because it is entirely unreliable in the real world of DUI investigations; however, it is very reliable in determining the mere presence of alcohol in the body. Thus, it is a good screening tool for probation departments and for minors where zero-tolerance is the rule. Although not invasive in the sense of a blood test, it is invasive of one's privacy as it requires an officer to watch the suspect urinate into a container to ensure the integrity of the sample. Urine is the substance of choice for drug testing purposes because drugs and their metabolites remain in the urine far longer than in the blood.

Be aware that some states, such as California, give the choice of type of test to the driver. Other states, such as Arizona, leave the choice to the officer. Multiple tests are authorized in many states. In other words, the officer may choose breath *and* blood, or multiples of the same type of chemical tests. In DUI homicide cases, it is not uncommon to see multiple blood draws at intervals of 15 minutes so that the government can establish an alcohol absorption or elimination curve for the arrestee.

B. Time of Driving vs. Time of Test

Obviously, when the police administer a chemical test it is not done while the suspect is driving—it is done at some point later in the investigation. Because of this, some jurisdictions require the government to prove the driver's BAC at the time of driving. This places the entire burden of proving that the alcohol absorption and elimination curves fall within known parameters so that the government's forensic toxicologist can extrapolate backward from the time of the chemical test to the time of driving. In this manner, the government's forensic toxicologist can proffer evidence that the driver was at or above a particular BAC while driving. A minority of states still have Time of Driving laws in place.

Many prosecutors became frustrated with this requirement that they prove that the driver had a BAC at or above the legal limit while driving. It simply made it too difficult to obtain convictions. Police, prosecuting agencies and private organizations lobbied the legislatures across the country to change the laws to put the burden on the defense. This became known as the *affirmative defense.*

The affirmative defense requires the defendant in a criminal case only to show some credible evidence that the driver's BAC *could* have been under the limit at the time of driving (not that it actually was under the legal limit). Once this occurs, the government must then prove that at the time of driving the defendant's BAC was at or above the per se level by proof beyond a reasonable doubt in order to win a conviction. The majority of states still have an affirmative defense.

Still unsatisfied with the difficulty of obtaining a conviction, police, prosecutors and private organizations lobbied state legislatures for laws that presume a driver's BAC to be as high as the chemical test result at the time of driving. Georgia led the way on this. Arizona and Washington soon followed and the domino effect has started. Under this scheme, it is illegal to drive with a prohibited BAC within a specified amount of time from the time of the stop. In other words, the law may state that it is illegal to drive if your BAC is .08 or more within two hours of driving—and it does not matter what the BAC was at the time of driving. Clearly this leads to prejudicial enforcement of the laws throughout jurisdictions with this scheme. If the driver blows a .065 twenty minutes after the stop of the vehicle, and .075 30 minutes after the stop, nothing will prevent the police from retesting the driver at 40 minutes and obtaining a BAC of .085.

C. Enhancements

A driver's BAC can lead to enhancements on sentencing and even to charges of new crimes. Some states have a graduated sentencing scheme where the punishment depends on the BAC level recorded by the police. In other words, a .08 to .099 would subject the violator to a lesser punishment than .10 or higher.

Some states have enacted completely separate laws for higher BACs. In other words, in a state where separate per se crimes are based on .08, .15 and .20, a driver who tests at .201 will be charged with four separate crimes: DUI, Driving with a BAC of .08 or More, Driving with a BAC of .15 or More, and Driving with a BAC of .20 or More.

While this multiple offense charging scheme seems to benefit the prosecution, in many instances it does not. Juries oftentimes feel as if they have to convict a person, despite a lack of evidence (simply because it is a DUI case). When multiple charges are brought, a jury may “split the baby” and convict only on the lesser charges.

Be careful when pleading to charges where BAC will make a difference in the sentence. One may be charged with per se violations of .08 and .15. If you have a recorded BAC of .175 and make a plea bargain to the .08 charge with the .15 charged being dismissed, you may still be liable for enhanced punishment (such as a mandatory ignition-interlock requirement) due to the higher BAC, never having been convicted of the .15 charge.

1.4 Drugged Driving Laws

Not many states have drugged-driving laws. Most are still exclusively alcohol-based laws; however the trend is changing rapidly. By the year 2020, I predict that all states will have drugged driving laws. Presently, drugged-driving laws mirror alcohol-based laws in that there are two categories: Impairment and Per Se.

A. Impairment

Drug-Impairment laws often mirror alcohol-impairment laws. However one clear distinction stands out in most states: many prescription and over-the-counter, legal drugs can impair your ability to drive, but there is usually a statutory exception for these drugs from a per se prosecution. But that does not mean that you can legally drive while impaired by one of these drugs. Hydrocodone may have been legally prescribed to you for pain, and you may be taking the prescribed dose, but if it impairs your ability to drive, then you may be prosecuted for DUI in many states.

Moreover, you may be taking a prescribed drug and have had some alcohol, but still be under your state’s per se BAC limit. Yet the combination of the alcohol, and drugs could render you impaired. This, too may be illegal. Many officers cannot discern a difference between alcohol impairment and drug impairment. Additionally, many officers cannot detect that you have even ingested some classes of drugs and will ask you if you have taken any drugs or medications. If you have ingested some, it is best to be silent about this issue.

B. Per Se

Per Se laws target illegal drugs, including prescription drugs taken without a prescription. States have taken varied approaches to per se drugged-driving laws.

The most strict of the states prohibit driving with any amount of an illegal drug in your body, or the drug's metabolite. Under this scheme, it does not matter if you are impaired. What matters is whether there is a detectable amount of the drug in your body. Necessarily, this means that one must consider the limits of scientific means of detection, but also the current acceptability of those limits within the relevant scientific community. Most states that have drugged-driving laws have taken a somewhat sensible approach, however, and have chosen a lower cut-off limit. The cut-off point is based on the limited, and sometimes unscientific, information regarding impairment levels due to drug-use.

Additionally, some states prohibit driving with the drug's metabolite in your system. Everything organic that we ingest is metabolized. Drugs are no exception. If you smoke marijuana today, the metabolites will still be in your system two weeks from today, although they certainly will have no effect on your ability to drive. Yet it still may be illegal to drive with them in your system. This is why it is very important to invoke your Miranda Rights at the time of a traffic stop or DUI investigation. You may have only had two beers and the police officer might let you go once his suspicions of DUI are resolved, but if you tell the officer that you smoked marijuana last week, he may arrest you and have you tested for presence of metabolites.

1.5 Boating Under the Influence

Boating Under the Influence (BUI) is codified in some states and left up to the discretion of officers and prosecutors as to whether it can be charged in other states. Important things to note are that there are no studies which correlate boating "behaviors" with a particular BAC, unlike driving a car. There is, however, one study on the effectiveness of Field Sobriety Testing (FST) done in 1990 and funded by NHTSA. An *Experimental Evaluation of a Field Sobriety Test Battery in a Marine Environment* evaluated such FSTs as The Walk-and-Turn, One Leg Stand, Horizontal Gaze Nystagmus, Finger Count, Finger to Nose, Hand Pat and Alphabet Recital.

The study found no significant lessening of the ability for the particular FST to determine whether someone was over or under a .10% BAC in a marine environment as opposed to on dry land. This conclusion is deceiving, however, as the last four FSTs mentioned have correlations to a BAC of .10% or more that are less than 50% (a coin toss is a better indicator). Moreover, the study is correlated to a .10%. We don't know what the correlation is when it is lowered to .08% (the latest Coast Guard standard). Additionally, officers believe that this study gives them license to administer FSTs on a rocking boat or floating dock and call the results "valid" indicators of impairment. It does not. FSTs should only be administered on a smooth, level, relatively hard and dry surface that does not move.

1.6 Flying Under the Influence

The circumstances surrounding the arrest for Flying Under the Influence (FUI) are almost always going to rely on someone reporting the pilot to local authorities. I have never heard of a pilot being "pulled over" by the police. These cases are going to rely heavily upon the circumstances under which the pilot is reported. In some cases, the pilot may be reported on the way to the aircraft and be arrested before he or she boards the plane. The question then becomes whether a crime actually occurred or not.

In any event, the rules of the Federal Aviation Administration will surely come into play in addition to any state laws. The FAA can be very harsh on pilots and the accused pilot can certainly lose his or her license to fly.

Chapter 2

DUI Stop and Arrest Procedures

2.1 Chapter Overview

This chapter explains what driving behaviors the police are trained to look for while on patrol. DUI Checkpoints (also known as "roadblocks") are discussed as well as Safe Harbor Laws. Miranda Rights are explained and Field Sobriety Testing is examined in detail. Most importantly, however, this chapter goes into great detail regarding what should happen at a typical DUI stop and investigation while giving advice as to what you could have done to give yourself the best chance of winning at trial.

2.2 Driving Behaviors that Attract Attention

The Fourth Amendment to the United States Constitution protects anyone within the United States from random, warrantless traffic stops. The police must have some legal reason to stop a motorist. This is quite different from an officer randomly approaching someone on foot and asking a few questions. On foot, however, you are always free to move on about your business while completely ignoring the officer.

Surprisingly, you can be stopped by the police for perfectly legal driving behavior and that traffic stop may hold up to constitutional scrutiny. For example, if a convenience store is robbed and a white '84 Chevrolet pickup with a dent in the passenger's side door was the getaway vehicle, and you happen to be driving an '84 Chevrolet pickup with a dent in the passenger's side door in the area, near the time of the robbery, you may be validly stopped by the police. Even though your driving behavior was not illegal in any manner, the police may stop you to alleviate their suspicions.

This type of reasoning has been extended to the DUI enforcement area. It is not illegal in any state to weave within your own lane without crossing any lane lines. Yet, if your vehicle is seen weaving within its lane, the police may be able to justify a traffic stop based on the suspicion that you are drunk.

The premier NHTSA publication on the subject of driving behavior *was* the *NHTSA Guide to Detecting Drunk Drivers at Night*. It listed 20 driving behaviors that police should look for when patrolling for DWI drivers at night. The *Guide* claims a correlation to a percentage chance that the driver is at or above .10 BAC and is invalid for daytime driving behaviors.

It has been replaced with the *NHTSA DWI Detection Guide*. The new guide now has 24 driving behaviors and has lost the requirement that the behaviors occur at night. There was no new research to support the four added behaviors or the loss of the nighttime requirement, yet the police prosecutors and many judges seem to ignore this. Moreover, the new definition of "DWI" is correlated to a .080.

The original study that led to both guides is titled *Visual Detection of Driving While Intoxicated*, by Douglas H. Harris, Anacapa Sciences, Inc. Santa Barbara, CA. ©1980 The Human Factors Society, Inc.

It is an eight-page study which first reviewed literature from other researchers on the issue of identifying DWI drivers, then involved ten law enforcement agencies throughout the United States which attempted to demonstrate the effectiveness of the identified visual cues. The stated purpose of the study was to research the effectiveness of DWI detection because it is "a function of the frequency with which patrol officers see and recognize cues indicative of DWI and the extent to which observed cues discriminate between DWI and driving while sober (DWS)."

The first issue noted in the study is that the author uses the terms DWI (Driving While Intoxicated) and DWS (Driving While Sober), yet the study itself is not correlated to sobriety or drunkenness; it is correlated to a specific blood alcohol level (BAC) and arrest rates. The study does not correlate to actual impairment or conviction rates. Moreover, the study concerns only those people driving at night—not during the daylight hours.

The study developed its own list of visual driving cues as well as reviewed lists of potential driving cues from a 1974 Michigan State University Study, *DWI Law Enforcement Training Project, Student Manual*, DOT Contract No. HS-334-3-645 by Carnahan, Holmes, Keyes, Stempler and Dreveskracht.

They analyzed 1,288 DWI arrest reports from nine agencies and found 3,658 visual detection cues. They prepared the data for analysis by dividing the cues into several categories and came up with a preliminary listing of 129 visual cues that they believed were useful for DWI detection. Think about it—129 visual cues are a staggering number and could cover almost every conceivable driving violation imaginable! In fact, some of the cues were not violations of the law at all. Take, for example, weaving within the lane. There are no statutes that make it illegal to use the entire lane.

There was a cumulative effect noted. Where two cues were seen together, 5% could be added to the percentage chance of DWI for the larger cue. If three or more were present, 10% could be added. The cumulative effect works as follows:

Drifting at night had a 45% correlation to .10 BAC or more.

Braking erratically at night had a 35% correlation to .10 BAC or more.

Where both drifting and erratic braking were seen in the same driver, the correlation was 50% to a BAC of .10 or more.

If we add in a third cue of turning with a wide radius at 60% for the same driver, the correlation would be 70%.

The current list of driving cues as published by NHTSA in the *DWI Detection Guide* can be divided into four categories: Maintaining Lane Position, Speed and Braking, Vigilance, and Judgment. These are the driving behaviors that the police are looking for.

A. Problems Maintaining Proper Lane Position

(50% alone or 75% when combined with any other cue)
Weaving, Weaving across lane lines, Straddling a lane line, Swerving, Turning with a wide radius, Drifting, Almost striking a vehicle or other object.

NHTSA describes the *Problems Maintaining Proper Lane Position* category on their website as follows:

> Maintaining proper lane position can be a difficult task for an impaired driver. For example, we have all seen vehicles weaving before. Weaving means that the vehicle alternately moves toward one side of the lane and then the other. The pattern of lateral movement can be fairly regular, as one steering correction is closely followed by another. In extreme cases, the vehicle's wheels even cross the lane lines before a correction is made. You might even observe a vehicle straddling a center or lane line. That is, the vehicle is moving straight ahead with either the right or left tires on the wrong side of the lane line or markers.
>
> Drifting means that a vehicle is moving in a generally straight line, but at a slight angle to the lane. The driver might correct his or her course as the vehicle approaches a lane line or other boundary, or fail to correct until after a boundary has been crossed. In extreme cases, the driver fails to correct in time to avoid a collision.
>
> Course corrections can be gradual or abrupt. For example, you might observe a vehicle to swerve, making an abrupt turn away from a generally straight course, when a driver realizes that he or she has

drifted out of proper lane position, or to avoid a previously-unnoticed hazard.

A related DWI cue is almost striking a vehicle or other object. You might observe a vehicle, either at slow speeds or moving with traffic, to pass unusually close to a sign, barrier, building, or other object. This cue also includes almost striking another vehicle, either moving or parked, and causing another vehicle to maneuver to avoid a collision.

Turning with a wide radius, or drifting during a curve, is the final cue in this category of driver behaviors. A vehicle appears to drift to the outside of the lane, or into another lane, through the curve or while turning a corner. Watch for this cue and stop the driver when you see it. Many alcohol-involved crashes are caused by an expanding turn radius, or drifting out of lane position during a curve.

B. Speed and Braking Problems

(45% alone or 70% when combined with any other cue)
Stopping problems (too far, too short, or too jerky), Accelerating or decelerating for no apparent reason, Varying speed, Slow speed (10+ mph under the limit)

NHTSA describes the *Speed and Braking Problems* category on their website as follows:

> The research showed that braking properly can be a difficult task for an impaired driver. For example, there is a good chance the driver is DWI if you observe any type of stopping problem. Stopping problems include; stopping too far from a curb or at an inappropriate angle, stopping too short or beyond a limit line, and jerky or abrupt stops.
>
> Impaired drivers also can experience difficulty maintaining an appropriate speed. There is a good chance the driver is DWI if you observe a vehicle to, accelerate or decelerate rapidly for no apparent reason, vary its speed, alternating between speeding up and slowing down, or be driven at a speed that is ten miles per hour or more under the limit.

C. Vigilance Problems

(55% alone or 65% when combined with any other cue)
Driving in opposing lanes or wrong way on one-way, Slow response to traffic signals, Slow or failure to respond to officer's signals, Stopping in lane for no apparent reason, Driving without headlights at night*, Failure to signal or signal inconsistent with action.*
(*50% when combined with any other cue).

NHTSA describes the *Vigilance Problems* category on their website as follows:

> Vigilance concerns a person's ability to pay attention to a task or notice changes in surroundings. A driver whose vigilance has been impaired by alcohol might forget to turn his or her headlights on when required.
>
> Similarly, impaired drivers often forget to signal a turn or lane change, or their signal is inconsistent with their maneuver, for example, signaling left, but turning right.
>
> Alcohol-impaired vigilance also results in motorists driving into opposing or crossing traffic, and turning in front of oncoming vehicles with an insufficient headway.
>
> Driving is a complex task that requires accurate information about surrounding traffic conditions. Failing to yield the right of way and driving the wrong way on a one way street are dangerous examples of vigilance problems.
>
> A driver whose vigilance has been impaired by alcohol also might respond more slowly than normal to a change in a traffic signal. For example, the vehicle might remain stopped for an unusually long period of time after the signal has turned green. Similarly, an impaired driver might be unusually slow to respond to an officer's lights, siren, or hand signals.
>
> The most extreme DWI cue in the category of vigilance problems is to find a vehicle stopped in a lane for no apparent reason. Sometimes when you observe this behavior the driver will be just lost or confused, but more than half of the time the driver will be DWI—maybe even asleep at the wheel.

D. Judgment Problems

(35% alone or 90% when combined with any other cue)
Following too closely, Improper or unsafe lane change, Illegal or improper turn (too fast, jerky, sharp, etc.), Driving on other than the designated roadway, Stopping inappropriately in response to officer, Inappropriate or unusual behavior (throwing, arguing, etc.), Appearing to be impaired

NHTSA describes the *Judgment Problems* category on their website as follows:

> Operating a motor vehicle requires continuous decision-making by the driver. Unfortunately, judgment abilities can be affected by even small amounts of alcohol. For example, alcohol-impaired judgment can

cause a driver to follow another vehicle too closely, providing an unsafe stopping distance.

Alcohol-impaired judgment also can result in a driver taking risks or endangering others. If you observe a vehicle to make improper or unsafe lane changes, either frequently or abruptly, or with apparent disregard for other vehicles, there is a good chance the driver's judgment has been impaired by alcohol.

Similarly, impaired judgment can cause a driver to turn improperly. For example, misjudgments about speed and the roadway can cause a driver to take a turn too fast, or to make sudden corrections during the maneuver. These corrections can appear to the observer as jerky or sharp vehicle movements during the turn.

Alcohol-impaired judgment can affect the full range of driver behaviors. For example, the research found that impaired drivers are less inhibited about making illegal turns than unimpaired drivers.

Driving on other than the designated roadway is another cue exhibited by alcohol-impaired drivers. Examples include driving at the edge of the roadway, on the shoulder, off the roadway entirely, and straight through turn-only lanes.

In some cases, impaired drivers stop inappropriately in response to an officer, either abruptly as if they had been startled, or in an illegal or dangerous manner.

In fact, the research has shown that there is a good chance a driver is DWI if you observe the person to exhibit any inappropriate or unusual behavior. Unusual behavior includes throwing something from the vehicle, drinking in the vehicle, urinating at the roadside, arguing with another motorist, or otherwise being disorderly. If you observe inappropriate or unusual behavior, there is a good probability that the driver is DWI.

Appearing to be Impaired: The final cue is actually one or more of a set of indicators related to the personal behavior or appearance of a driver. These indicators include, gripping the steering wheel tightly, driving with one's face close to the windshield, slouching in the seat, and staring straight ahead with eyes fixed. Some officers routinely scrutinize the faces of drivers in oncoming traffic, looking for the indicators of impairment. If you observe a driver who appears to be impaired, the research showed that there is an excellent probability that you are correct in your judgment.

One can visit the NHTSA website and find explanations for the 24 driving cues. The NHTSA website general address is www.nhtsa.com

and the web address which will take you directly to the driving cues is: www.nhtsa.dot.gov/people/injury/alcohol/dwi/dwihtml/index.htm

E. Detecting Impaired Motorcyclists

There is a separate class of driving behaviors that the police look for with motorcyclists. In fact, there is a special guide for motorcyclists, separate and apart from the *DWI Detection Guide*. The impetus claimed by NHTSA for the motorcycle guide (not the study), *The Detection of DWI Motorists* (U.S. Department of Transportation, National Highway Traffic Safety Administration DOT HS 807 856, Revised; March, 2005), was the NHTSA estimate that in 2003, 36 percent of motorcycle operators who were involved in fatal crashes had a BAC of 0.01 or higher. Remember that 0.01 BAC in a 150-lb. male is less than one drink and there is very limited data to suggest that a BAC of .01 will produce any effects of impairment in a human being. Moreover, the phrase "motorcycle operators who were involved in fatal crashes" does not necessarily mean that the operator of the motorcycle was impaired. The phrase easily encompasses sober motorcyclists who were hit by drunk automobile drivers. Based on this, however, NHTSA concluded:

> "Clearly, enforcing impaired driving laws is a key to reducing the number of alcohol-related motorcyclist fatalities. *But which cues should be used to detect impaired motorcyclists?*"

NHTSA sponsored a study published long before the Guide, in 1993, which interviewed police officers and examined 1,000 arrest reports (*The Detection of DWI Motorcyclists*, DOT HS 807 839, March 1993; Jack W. Stuster, Anacapa Sciences, Inc.). They did field evaluations in two separate studies and they eventually narrowed a list over about 100 cues down to fourteen cues, seven of which they claim are "excellent" predictors of impairment and the remaining seven as "good" predictors of impairment.

What does NHTSA mean by "excellent" predictors? They mean 50% or greater—somewhere from a coin-flip and up.

What does NHTSA mean by "good" predictor? They mean 30% to 50%—less than the probability of a coin toss.

Clearly, from the lack of evidence showing that anyone is impaired at a 0.01 BAC and their labeling of "good" predictors and "excellent" predictors which amount to the probability of a coin toss, there is fertile ground for attacking the NHTSA motorcycle cues in court. The guide published by NHTSA gives ample ammunition for cross examination. Page 3 of the guide states:

> "…some officers, even those with many years of experience, reported they believe there are no cues that can be used to distinguish DWI from unimpaired motorcycle operation."

The driving behaviors that the police look for with motorcyclists are:

Excellent Cues (50% or greater probability)

- Drifting during a turn or curve
- Trouble with a dismount
- Trouble with balance at a stop
- Turning problems (unsteady, sudden corrections, late braking, improper lean angle)
- Inattentive to surroundings
- Inappropriate or unusual behavior (carrying or dropping an object, urinating at roadside, disorderly conduct)
- Weaving

Good Cues (30% to 49% probability)

- Erratic movement while going straight
- Operating without lights at night
- Recklessness
- Following too closely
- Running stop light or sign
- Evasion
- Wrong way

If we deconstruct the cues listed above, it becomes more than clear that they run the gambit from highly objective to highly subjective. Obviously, driving the wrong way on a one-way street, running a stop sign/light or riding without lights on at night would be highly objective. Weaving, following too closely or erratic movements are toward the middle of the spectrum. Finally, trouble with balance/dismount, recklessness and inattentiveness to surroundings are most subjective. View, however, the cue labeled "carrying an object." NHTSA claims that this is a cue. But motorcycles certainly have limited storage space so sometimes it is a necessity for a driver to carry an object. Does lack of storage space create a cue?

Moreover, the "evasion" cue either is speculative or should be renamed "attempted evasion" because anyone who evaded the officers would not have his or her BAC measured to contribute to the study.

There were some cues that had a high correlation in the study, but did not make it into the final guide. Among the cues was pushing a motorcycle either on or off road. This cue had the same probability that a motorcyclist was .05–.09; .10 to .14; and .15 to .19 as did striking an object while riding. Perhaps it was not included because the motorcyclist was not actually riding.

Likewise riding a stolen motorcycle had predictors as high as or higher than some cues that actually made it into the guide. Failure to pay a toll, coasting downhill, "wearing silly headgear" and a category called "facial expression" all had high correlations yet did not make the final guide.

Finally, note that the published guide for automobile drivers at least claims to correlate to a percentage probability that the driver is at or above a particular BAC. The published motorcycle guide makes no such claims—they simply predict that the driver is "DWI" without defining "DWI" in terms of a BAC.

2.3 Roadblocks

The police, prosecutors and right-wing judges call them "Sobriety Checkpoints," but I prefer to call them what they are: "Roadblocks." How we as a free society came to allow the random, warrantless and suspicionless stop of travelers on public roadways to see ***if*** they have committed a crime is beyond me. One word can sum up the efficacy of roadblocks—*ineffective*. One word can sum up my opinion of the constitutionality of roadblocks—*unconstitutional*. Unfortunately, the United States Supreme Court does not share my view.

What can you expect when driving up to a roadblock? First there will be signs advertising the existence of the roadblock as you approach. The signs may read: "Sobriety Checkpoint Ahead." In order to be legal, the checkpoint must leave the driver an exit route, so that the driver may avoid the roadblock altogether. However, the exit route need not be reasonable. For instance, the roadblock signs may be placed so that the only way to avoid the roadblock is to turn onto a dead-end street off of a one-way road. Thus, if you turn onto the dead-end road, your only choice is to park and remain there until the roadblock closes and all of the police have left, or to turn around and proceed back through the roadblock.

As you approach, there will be much activity, road flares may be present, along with high-intensity floodlights illuminating the area. A police officer or police auxiliary volunteer will approach the car and either wave you through, or stop you and ask questions. It is important to note that the police are prohibited from stopping people based on anything but a random count of cars. In other words, the police must have a plan to stop every car, every other car, every fifth car, etc. However, don't be surprised when the police suddenly shift from every third car to every car when a non-white driver or a car full of teenagers approaches the roadblock.

The government agent stopping the car will tell you that you were stopped as part of a sobriety checkpoint and ask if you have had anything to drink. I recommend answering the government agent through the window of the car and not putting it down, or staying completely silent at this point. Simply do not answer the question. Ask if you are free to go.

If they tell you that you are not free to go, ask what you are being arrested for. They will likely tell you that you are being investigated. Ask to leave, but do not run. If you run, they will chase you and could quite possibly hurt you.

If they ask you to get out of the car, do so, but refuse to do any Field Sobriety Tests unless and until you have spoken to your attorney.

Complain about roadblocks to your local law enforcement, judges and city or town councils. Write letters to everyone that you can think of in authority to express your displeasure with the fact that your liberty was violated by uniformed officers who had no reason to stop you. The Constitution is only alive if we take the time to enforce it.

2.4 Safe Harbor Laws

Safe Harbor Laws refer to the situation where a driver feels as if he has had too much to drink to drive and either decides to use his car as a stationary shelter to sleep it off, having never moved the vehicle, or where the driver decides to pull over and remain in the vehicle until sober.

There is an important difference between the two scenarios. In the first scenario, the "driver" never really was a driver. In the second scenario, the driver likely broke the impairment laws before he relinquished control. In the second scenario, if the police can prove that the driver drove to the spot where he elected to stop, he may not be insulated from prosecution. This is why it is imperative that when you are approached by the police in this situation, that you invoke your Miranda Rights and remain silent. Oftentimes police will ask you how you got to the location and you will admit to having driven there. Facts can be very easily twisted by the police and prosecution to infer that you drove there while drunk. For example, a man drives to a bar, drinks to the point of intoxication, then decides to sleep it off in his car at the bar. The police arrive and interrogate the drunken suspect who agrees that he drove to that location. A skilled prosecutor can then take those facts and twist them leading to the conviction of an innocent man. When the accused takes the stand at trial to profess his innocence and claim that he did not drink until after he drove to the bar, the prosecutor can argue that the accused said nothing of that when he was arrested.

Safe Harbor Laws are under attack in every state. Political lobby groups have pressured lawmakers to change safe harbor laws to convict innocent people who are trying to act in a responsible manner. Original safe harbor laws in most states required a driver to remove his vehicle from the traveled portion of the roadway, turn it off and remove the keys from the ignition. If the prosecution could not prove that the person drove to that location while impaired, then the person was insulated from prosecution.

Some states, like Maryland, realized that the occupant of the vehicle might need to operate some of the controls of the vehicle in order to stay warm, or to call for help. They adopted a very reasonable approach which allows a jury to consider whether the driver was simply using the vehicle as a stationary shelter, or whether the driver posed a risk to the public by exercise of present or imminent physical control of the vehicle (*Atkinson v. State of Maryland*, 627 A.2d 1019, 1993).

States seem to be moving away from the reasonable approach, however, and making it a crime if the driver has the ability to put the vehicle into the flow of traffic. Thus, a driver may no longer be insulated from prosecution if he follows the bright-line rule of parking the vehicle and removing the key from the ignition. Moreover, technology seems to have out-paced the laws once more. Some new cars do not require a key in an ignition switch to start the car, just the push of a start button.

Perhaps the worst of the safe harbor laws comes from an Arizona decision called *State v. Vermuele*, 160 Ariz. 295, 772 P.2d 1148 (Ariz.App. 1989). This case makes bad public policy. The court held that there was actual physical control because the defendant voluntarily placed himself behind the wheel and placed his key in the ignition and turned it to the "on" position so that he could use his cell phone to call for a ride. The court wrote: "Here, there is no question that appellee, who was not asleep, and who had placed the keys of his vehicle into the ignition and turned it as far as the "on" position, was readily capable of placing his vehicle into the stream of traffic. It is clear that appellee was in "actual physical control" of his vehicle, and the officers would have been derelict in their duties had they allowed appellee to start the engine and begin operating the vehicle." Yet they ignored the fact that his actions were to allow him to power a cell phone to call for a ride.

2.5 DUI on Private Property

Private property is no longer a safe haven in most states. In the past, a DUI could only occur on a public roadway. Now, however, some states can charge people with DUI when it occurs "anywhere in the state." The need for this is obvious when one considers that people can be charged with boating and flying under the influence. A minority of states require that a DUI occur on a public roadway or where the public frequently travels.

2.6 The DUI Traffic Stop

A. What to Expect and What to Do

The traffic stop will most often start with a patrol car following you and using emergency equipment to signal you to stop. Most often, the police will use just flashing red and blue lights to stop you, but some also use a siren as a matter of course. The vast majority of DUI stops occur at night.

Local laws everywhere require a driver to pull to the right side of the road. It is often a good idea to get out of the flow of traffic for your own safety, which is why police often prefer that you pull into a parking lot or onto a side-street. You should look for a well-lit area to stop, but this is a double-edged sword. If you do not pull off into the first-available area and wait for a well-lit place, the prosecutor will claim that you were too drunk to realize that you were being stopped. If you stop at the first available place, but it is dark, you might be putting yourself at risk because of the surroundings. There are reports from every part of the country in which people have been assaulted by someone pretending to be a police officer with red and blue lights in the grill of an "unmarked" patrol car.

Expect the officer to focus the patrol car's spotlight on your side-view mirror or the rearview mirror. This does two things. First, it reflects light into the cab of your vehicle, making it more easy for the officer to see what you are doing. Second, it provides a "curtain of light" so that you are temporarily blinded and the officer can approach without you having a clear view of him. This comes into play when the officer later testifies that you were slow to exit the vehicle and seemed unsure of your steps as you walked to the rear of your car at his direction. Clearly, this is because you have just been temporarily blinded by a very powerful spotlight, but police and prosecutors will use it to claim that you were drunk.

Everyone is nervous when being stopped by the police. It is important to keep your hands in plain view when the officer approaches. The steering wheel is a good place to keep your hands to appear non-threatening. Always try to remember that a traffic stop is among the more dangerous of police activities because the police do not know if they will be simply issuing a civil traffic ticket to a motorist, or suddenly dealing with an armed individual who is on the FBI's Most-Wanted List.

The officer will stand slightly behind the driver's side door. This allows the officer to look over your shoulder and makes it more difficult for you to point a weapon at him. The officer will probably ask you for your license, insurance and registration at some point during the initial contact. Officers are trained to watch how you retrieve the documents. This is a *divided attention task* (see Field Sobriety Testing, below). It is a smart idea to keep your current registration and insurance card together, in one envelope, in an easily accessible place. Police are known to claim that a driver seemed impaired because it took him a long time to find the vehicle's registration, or because he forgot one of the documents. Also, it is a good idea to keep your driver's license in an easily-accessible portion of your wallet or purse. Police will often testify that one's ability to smoothly retrieve a license from a wallet is a sign of impairment, when it is really nothing more than a sign of a tight pocket within the wallet.

The officers are trained to ask you distracting questions while they watch you retrieve your documents such as: Where are you going? Are you familiar with the area? Is this your car? These questions are designed to make you lose focus on what you were doing. Another important question that the officer should ask is: Do you know why I stopped you?

A driver should never answer this question. The officer is doing two things. He is fishing for more information and he is trying to get you to admit to a legitimate reason for the traffic stop. For example, a driver may have run a stop sign without the officer seeing it. The officer makes a traffic stop based on an expired registration and asks the driver if she knows why she was stopped. The driver says that it was probably because she ran a stop sign. The officer, without missing a beat, says: "Yes—*and* because your registration is expired."

If you were stopped for speeding, the officer will ask if you knew how fast you were going and if you know what the speed limit is in that area. Many people think that ignorance will get them out of the ticket. They think that if they tell the officer that they did not know their speed, or the speed limit, the officer will realize that they did not intend to speed, and not write a ticket. As a result, many people will tell the officer that they did not know how fast they were going and that they did not know what the speed limit was in the area. Later, when they try to fight the ticket in court and they suddenly "regain" their memory ("Your Honor, I was doing 40 miles per hour—the posted speed limit") the testimony is far less than credible. Ignorance is not a defense.

My advice is to remain completely and utterly silent. Silence will never get you into any more trouble than your mouth will, and it will probably result in far less trouble. You must still present the documents requested by the officer, but you do not have to say anything to the officer. Remember this: the police officer is not your friend in this situation. The officer is trying to gather as much evidence against you as possible. This evidence will be used to convict you of a criminal offense.

Another advantage to remaining completely silent is that it is very disconcerting to the officer. I advise people not to even look at the officer. Keep your head and eyes down. Police are trained to deal with polite people, nervous people, belligerent and violent people. They are not trained to deal with people who ignore them, but are compliant. When you remove the officer from his training and make him go "off script," you have gained the advantage. If you have a passenger, tell him or her to shut up and stay in the car unless the officer asks that person to step out.

The officer will likely ask if you have been drinking. Do not lie to the officer. Lying to the police is illegal and it is quite likely that they will be able to show that you have been drinking at some point, which means that you are a liar. Liars don't often fair well in front of a jury. The proper thing to do when the officer asks if you have been drinking is to remain completely silent.

The officer will likely ask you to get out of the car and he will watch every move as you do so. At a traffic stop, you must get out upon request of the officer. Do not use the door of the car, the roof, or the frame for support as you get out. If you do not get out, you may be forcibly removed from the car at some point and the police may hurt you in the process. Be wary that some officers delight in hurting people when they have the opportunity. Many police have joined the force not because they want to help people, but because they get a rush and an undue sense of self-importance by having authority.

The officer will ask you to perform some Field Sobriety Tests (FSTs). You should simply not comply. Do not refuse verbally, simply stand with your arms at your sides and look at your feet. Do not acknowledge the officer. Nowhere in the country are you required to do FSTs. About the worst thing that can happen by not doing the FSTs is that the prosecutor may be able to use your refusal against you as evidence of guilt. In some jurisdictions, they may not even be able to do that.

People think that they can pass an FST. This is false. No one can pass an FST. The results of an FST are either "failure" or "inconclusive" (see Field Sobriety Testing section below for a thorough explanation of this concept). If you perform the FST perfectly, the result is inconclusive. If you decline to take the FST, the result is inconclusive.

The officer may want you to answer some questions. You should refuse to answer any questions by remaining completely silent. Do not acknowledge the officer. Now the officer has a choice: arrest you or let you go.

If the officer arrests you, rest assured that he was going to arrest you whether you did the FSTs and answered questions, or not. The officer must justify his arrest with probable cause. Police build probable cause in a DUI case by putting together driving behavior, your statements, signs and symptoms of alcohol consumption and the results of FSTs. By being non-compliant and silent, you have removed statements, FSTs and the ubiquitous "slurred speech" component of probable cause.

If the officer reads you your Miranda warnings, you need do nothing to invoke them. You can simply remain silent. I recommend that you ask for an attorney. This is only one of two times that you should break your silence. You should say: "I want an attorney, now." Anything other than an unequivocal and direct request for an attorney may be ignored by the police.

Miranda Rights are as follows:

You have the right to remain silent.
Anything you say can, and will, be used against you in a court of law.
You have the right to have an attorney present with you prior to and during questioning if you so desire.
If you cannot afford an attorney, one will be appointed to you.
Do you understand your rights?

Some police ask you if you will waive your rights and answer questions.

Miranda Rights are only required where you are not free to go and the police are asking you questions about a crime. Some people are arrested and are never read their rights. This is perfectly acceptable if the police do not ask the person any questions. The important things to understand about the protections offered by Miranda Rights are as follows:

If you invoke your Miranda Rights and do not answer questions, a jury will never find out that you did so. Think about it—it always looks bad if you are accused of a crime and do not try to explain your innocence to the police. But courts understand this and have held that the government cannot hold your invocation of constitutional rights against you.

Likewise, the jury will never find out that you asked to speak to an attorney. Again, this is your constitutional right and it cannot be held against you.

Any statements that you make, even after being read Miranda Rights, are fair game. That is why you should always remain silent. Never try to explain the events or talk your way out of anything. Chances are, you will simply be digging yourself a hole. When you invoke your Miranda Rights, it does not mean that the police cannot ask you questions. It simply means that you have the right to remain silent. If you start answering questions after the police have read you your Miranda Rights, those answers are admissible as evidence against you.

Miranda Rights only apply when you are in custody. Oftentimes, when people are stopped by the police and asked if they have had anything to drink, the answer is admissible in court. This is because at the initial traffic stop, the law does not consider the driver to be "in custody" for purposes of Miranda. A police officer can walk up to you on the street and ask you a question about a crime. If you give an incriminating response, it will not be protected by Miranda. In non-

DUI investigations, it is quite common for a police investigator to call a suspect on the phone and ask incriminating questions while recording the conversation. There is no way that anyone could reasonably argue that Miranda Rights should apply since the suspect could always simply hang up the phone.

Miranda is not a license to lie. If you made statements which are suppressed (i.e. a jury cannot be told of them) and you take the stand in your own defense, the prosecutor can ask you the same questions as the police asked. In other words, if you told the police that you drank two 6-packs of beer and that statement is thrown out because of a Miranda violation, you probably should not testify at trial. If you do, the prosecutor may ask you how many drinks you had. If you reply that you had only two beers, the previously inadmissible "two 6-pack" statement may be used against you.

Once you are placed under arrest, you may be required to submit to a chemical test such as breath, blood or urine or any combination of the tests. This is where state laws vary greatly. In some states, you are not required to submit to any chemical testing while in other states, chemical testing is a requirement by statute. Some states require an affirmative statement that you will submit to chemical testing. If you are in a state that requires an affirmative statement, and you choose to follow the law, the only thing that you need to say when the officer asks if you will submit to testing is "yes."

If you refuse to submit to a test, you could be charged with a crime. Many states require a driver license suspension for refusal to submit to a test. Some states will allow the issuance of a search warrant for a forcible blood draw or (as in Arizona) for a forced catheterization for a urine test. The common denominator in all states is that the refusal to test may be used as evidence of guilt.

After the chemical test, the police may release you or book you. If you are booked, you may have to post bail, or you may be released by a judge of your own recognizance (R.O.R.). Whether you make bail or are released R.O.R., you will have to attend a court date sometime in the near future. Be sure that you are aware of the date and attend it.

Your car may be stored at the scene or the police may allow a sober driver designated by you to drive it away. It may also be towed and impounded. Local laws, police agency policy and the predilections of the arresting officer will govern what happens to your car.

If you are released to a sober friend, or if they call a taxi for you, do not return to your car. I have seen many people who are released and then return to their car to drive it home. Police are known to await a returning driver and then swoop in to make a second arrest when that person starts the car.

2.7 Field Sobriety Testing

A. What are Field Sobriety Tests?

The short answer to this question is that they are a method police and prosecutors use to justify your conviction. Field Sobriety Tests (FSTs) and Standardized Field Sobriety Tests (SFSTs) are divided attention tasks. Divided Attention Tasks ask you to focus your attention on more than one requirement. For example, the One Leg Stand FST requires you to simultaneously remember a set of instructions, while balancing on one leg, while counting out loud, while keeping your arms at your sides, while not swaying or hopping or putting your foot down for 30 seconds. The inability to divide your attention between these tasks supposedly correlates to a particular blood alcohol concentration on some divided attention tasks. Other divided attention tasks have never been correlated to any BAC.

It is important to realize that you cannot pass an FST. Think of failure as a correlation to a particular illegal BAC. If you do everything right on the FST, there is no correlation to a legal BAC or soberness. The result is inconclusive. Thus, one cannot "pass" an FST. The result is either failure or inconclusive.

Many tests have been suggested and tested for police to use to determine whether to arrest a suspected DUI driver or let her or him go free. The National Highway Traffic Safety Administration (NHTSA) has spent millions of tax dollars on grants to determine which tests are the most effective for law enforcement purposes. NHTSA settled on a three-test battery which they recommend for use by law enforcement. The tests are Horizontal Gaze Nystagmus (HGN), Walk-and-Turn (WAT), and One-Leg-Stand (OLS). NHTSA claims that these tests are both "Standardized" and "Validated."

Many times these terms are confused and incorrectly interchanged. The term "standardized" refers to a method of administering and interpreting the SFSTs. Standardized tests are supposed to be administered and interpreted in the same manner and under the same conditions no matter where they take place. The theory is that a police officer in New York should be able to administer the tests and interpret them in the same manner as an officer in California. Standardization is not a complex issue. We live with standardization in many respects. For example, copy paper is standardized at 8.5 x 11 inches, EXIT signs are standardized as to color and size, even fast-food is standardized. In fact, one could standardize the way one puts on shoes and socks in the morning by simply doing it the same way, every day, without change. Cronbach (1970) defines a standardized test as being "one in which the procedures, apparatus, and scoring have been fixed so that precisely the same testing procedures can be followed at different times and places." Cronbach, L., *Essentials of Psychological Testing*, New York: Harper & Row, 1970.

The term "validated" refers to the correlation between performance on an SFST and a particular Blood Alcohol Content (BAC). Contrary to what the prosecution says in virtually every state across the nation, the SFSTs have no correlation to impairment. They merely (and crudely) predict BAC. Moreover, there is no "pass" or "fail" with regard to FSTs. However, some police and prosecutors will consistently use those terms to describe a suspect's performance on FSTs. Also, don't confuse the term "validated" with the term "valid." As previously mentioned, "validated" is the term used by the authors of the studies to describe a correlation to a particular BAC. "Valid" has the connotation of truth. Prosecutors and police often attempt to portray SFSTs as valid indicators of impairment, when they are not.

If you want to do your own research, there are six major studies regarding FSTs:

1. Title: *Psychophysical Tests for DWI Arrests*
Authors: Marcelline Burns and Herbert Moskowitz, 132 pages
June 1977
Performing Organization: Southern California Research Institute
Department of Transportation Number DOT HS 802 424

2. Title: *Development & Field Test of Psychophysical Tests for DWI Arrests*
Authors: V. Tharp, Marcelline Burns and Herbert Moskowitz, 98 pages.
March 1981
Performing Organization: Southern California Research Institute
Department of Transportation Number DOT HS 805 864

3. Title: *Field Evaluation of a Behavioral Test Battery for DWI*
Authors: Theodore E. Anderson, Robert M. Schweitz, and Monroe B. Snyder
September 1983
Performing Organization: Office of Driver and Pedestrian Research, Problem-Behavior Research Division
Department of Transportation Number DOT HS 806 475

4. Title: *A Colorado Validation Study of the Standardized Field Sobriety Test (SFST) Battery*
Authors: Ellen Anderson and Marcelline Burns
November 1995, Second Printing: September 1996.
Performing Organization: Southern California Research Institute
Department of Transportation Number: None

5. Title: *Validation of the Standardized Field Sobriety Test Battery at BACs Below .10 Percent*
Authors: Jack Stuster and Marcelline Burns
San Diego, August 1998
Performing Organization: ANACAPA Sciences, Inc.
Department of Transportation Number: DOT HS 808 839

6. Title: *A Florida Validation Study of the Standardized Field Sobriety Test (S.F.S.T.) Battery*
Authors: Marcelline Burns
Florida, 1997
Performing Organization: Institute of Police Technology and Management, University of North Florida, Pinellas County Sheriff's Office, Southern California Research Institute
Department of Transportation Number: None

The studies are analyzed and evaluated below:

ANALYSIS: THE 1977 SCRI STUDY

1. Psychophysical Tests for DWI Arrests, June 1977
Authors: Marcelline Burns and Herbert Moskowitz, 132 pages
Performing Organization: Southern California Research Institute
Department of Transportation Number DOT HS 802 424

More commonly known as simply "The 1977 Study," this is the original study on SFSTs. It was prepared for the U.S. Department of Transportation, National Highway Traffic Safety Administration under contract number DOT-HS-5-01242. The study was conducted from June 30, 1975 to February 28, 1977 which is a 20-month period.

The primary focus of the study was to evaluate then-used police sobriety tests and to develop more sensitive and reliable measures. Standardization was also a stated purpose.

Ten police officers administered six tests to 238 participants who were light, moderate and heavy drinkers. BACs ranged from zero to .150%. Some participants received placebo drinks. Officers scored the participants on a 1–10 scale, basing an arrest/release decision on the entire six-test battery. The correlation was to a BAC of .10%. There were 168 men and 70 women. Their ages ranged from 20 to 71 years old, with an average age of 26 years, 6 months. Of the participants, 62 were classified as light drinkers, 86 as moderate and 90 as heavy drinkers.

The six-test battery comprised the Walk-and-Turn (WAT), One-Leg-Stand (OLS), Alcohol Gaze Nystagmus (AGN—not administered exactly as the more recently known test: "HGN"), Tracing and alternate tests such as Romberg Body Sway, Subtraction, Counting Backward, and Letter Cancellation.

All tests were found to be alcohol sensitive to one degree or another. The officers made a correct arrest/release decision 76% of the time. The "best" battery of tests was found to be the 3-test battery of AGN, Walk-and-Turn, and One-Leg-Stand commonly used by officers today. The study found that the 3-test battery of HGN can be administered in less than 5 minutes at roadside with an almost 84% accuracy rate. The tests can be adapted for a more accurate evaluation if done at the station in a more controlled environment. The officers made the correct decision to release the subject 73% of the time. The study notes that officers indicated that they would have arrested 101 people, 47 of whom had BACs below .10%. Of special note is the fact that there were 6 subjects who had no alcohol at all, but officers indicated that they would have arrested them anyway. Research observers indicated that they would have arrested one of the same six. The study faults itself for the fact that the police may have been more likely to make an "arrest" in the laboratory situation than in the field because of the negative consequences of a false arrest. The researchers stated: "In actual practice, the most common error at roadside is a false negative; unless an officer has a high degree of certainty that an individual's BAC is over .10%, he is most likely to release rather than arrest." Yet the researchers give no basis for this statement, which DUI Defense Attorneys all over the country know, anecdotally, to be false.

The authors state that the study shows that "substantial impairment typically occurs at a BAC lower than .10%, the current arbitrarily defined level for DWI arrest." The authors suggest a "more appropriate" legal limit of .08%.

Test subjects were instructed not to eat or use any stimulants for four hours prior to testing and they were to arrive alcohol-free. These conditions were violated by a number of subjects and some even arrived with positive BACs. The violations were ignored by the researchers.

The final test battery of AGN, Walk-and-Turn and One-Leg-Stand was chosen not only because of the individual reliability of the results, but also because they could be used in the field with little or no specialized equipment and because they did not take an inordinate amount of time to complete. Of special note, however, is that tracing was the second most accurate test next to nystagmus when single-test data was examined.

It is important to note that comparison for a relationship to driving impairment was never made with actual driving. The researcher used only visual tracking and other non-driving-based tests for comparison. The researchers did not develop any new tests at all and only correlated the results to a BAC above or below .10%. And, finally, they did standardize the tests and observation procedures.

2. Development & Field Test of Psychophysical Tests for DWI Arrests, March 1981

Title: *Development & Field Test of Psychophysical Tests for DWI Arrests*
Authors: V. Tharp, Marcelline Burns and Herbert Moskowitz, 98 pages.
Performing Organization: Southern California Research Institute
Department of Transportation Number DOT HS 805 864

This is probably the most important SFST study done. It serves as the basis for the 3-test battery of HGN, Walk-and-Turn and One-Leg-Stand and its results have been quoted in every NHTSA SFST Manual to date. Studies prior to this one served as the basis for this study and those since have only reinterpreted the findings.

The administration and scoring procedures for the 3-test battery of the HGN, Walk-and-Turn and One-Leg-Stand were standardized for this study. The battery was examined in the laboratory and, to a limited extent, in the field. The study was started in August of 1978 and ended in March 1981.

Ten officers from Los Angeles area police agencies examined 297 drinking volunteers in the lab from 0% BAC to .18% BAC. There were 202 male subjects and 95 females. One of the female subjects became ill during the research and was unable to return for the second round of testing. None of the laboratory subjects was under 21 years of age and only two were 65 or older.

Officers in the lab were able to correctly classify 81% of the volunteers as above or below .10% BAC.

In the field, officers filled out 3,128 data forms, each representing a driver stopped within a 3-month period. The forms included an estimate of the driver's BAC. Drivers who were released were breath-tested, anonymously.

As in the 1977 study, participants were asked no to eat, or drink, or use drugs prior to their arrival at the testing facility. Not all complied with those instructions. In fact, three subjects arrived with BACs of .05% or more. Illicit drug use was a major concern of the researchers as they did not want any cumulative effect of drugs and alcohol to skew their results. No drug testing was performed to rule out the possible effects of any drugs on the results. The researchers administered an HGN test to the subjects to check for drug use. Those people who displayed moderate to strong nystagmus at maximum deviation were given placebo doses of alcohol. These people were classified as being high-risk for a false positive result—in other words, the police might see the nystagmus and improperly classify the subject as being over .10%. One of these individuals, even though at a zero

BAC, was classified as being over .10% by the police and four other subjects at a zero BAC were classified as being over .10% by research staff.

The researchers also relied on the truthfulness of the subjects to report any illegal drug use in a study which used police officers to test the subjects.

Walk-and-Turn: Results for the Walk-and-Turn test showed that asking the subject to balance heel-to-toe while listening to instructions increased the sensitivity to alcohol. Asking people to watch their feet while performing the test also increased sensitivity to alcohol, but made the test difficult for people with monocular vision and poor depth perception. Performing the test with one's eyes open with enough light to see a frame of reference was essential if sober participants were to perform the test without difficulty. The study also found that people over 65 years of age, people with back, leg or middle-ear problems and people wearing high-heeled shoes (over 2 inches) had difficulty performing the tests even when sober. The researched recommended that only the HGN test be used with people over 65, back, leg or middle-ear problems and that those wearing high-heeled shoes be asked to remove them.

One-Leg-Stand: Few variables were found to alter the sensitivity of the One-Leg-Stand test. It was found that a subject at a BAC of .10% might keep balance for 20–25 seconds, but would likely falter after that point. The officer must ask the subject to count from 1001 to 1030 in order to estimate the passage of 30 seconds. Yet the standardization states that the officer is to ask the subject to count "rapidly" from 1001 to 1030 and nowhere in the instructions does the officer tell the subject to estimate the passage of 30 seconds.

More important, however, is that the study found that the subject must be able to see in order to orient himself or herself and that the police must stand back from the subject in order not to provide an artificial frame of reference which could distract the subject. The study clearly states: "Generally, if the stopee cannot see or orient with respect to a perpendicular frame of reference, then this test will be difficult to perform even if sober."

Experience tells us that if we ask an officer whether he or she gave the defendant a perpendicular or vertical frame of reference to guide from while doing the test, the officer will generally say "no," fearing that he or she administered the test in the wrong manner. This gives the defense attorney ample opportunity to impeach the officer with the study.

The study also found that certain individuals will have difficulty performing this test under sober conditions. Those people over 65 years of age, people with back, leg or middle-ear problems, people 50 lbs. or more overweight and people wearing high-heeled shoes (over 2 inches) had difficulty performing the tests even when sober. The research recommended that only the HGN test be used with such people and that those wearing high-heeled shoes be asked to remove them. The researchers state: "These individuals should only be given the nystagmus test."

The One-Leg-Stand test should be performed only on a hard, dry, level, non-slippery surface under relatively safe conditions. Note that the research requires a level surface—not "relatively level," or "level-enough" as some officers testify is the requirement. Oftentimes, all it takes is an investigator with a level and a camera to show just how bad the conditions were for this test.

"Relatively safe conditions" can certainly be argued to exclude tests conducted by the side of a busy interstate highway or where there is any chance of being struck by passing traffic.

Horizontal Gaze Nystagmus: There is a strong correlation between the angle of onset and BAC. As the angle of onset decreases, the BAC increases.

In the pilot study there were a number of variables found not to affect the test: stimulus brightness, room brightness, fixation distance, velocity of the stimulus movement, monocular versus binocular fixation, instructions to inhibit nystagmus and the vertical positioning of the eyes. Some of the variables, however, were found to be important in aiding the observer to record the nystagmus. For example, if done in poorly lit conditions, a flashlight must be used to illuminate the subject's eyes. The stimulus must be held slightly above eye-level in order to reduce squinting and allow the observer to clearly see the eye movements.

The researchers found that the gaze nystagmus test may not be applicable to certain individuals. People wearing hard contact lenses may not be able to complete the test because it requires lateral eye movement that may be inhibited by the lenses. Also, about 3% of the population will show early-onset nystagmus, and impaired balance, with no alcohol in their systems. This could be due to drugs other than alcohol, brain damage, illness, or of unknown cause.

The study found, "Since police officers often arrest intoxicated individuals after midnight, possible effects of fatigue or circadian rhythms on gaze nystagmus could be significant." It was found that the angle of onset after midnight was decreased in a segment of the participants.

They also found that while speed of the stimulus is not critical, if the speed drops below 10 degrees per second while looking for the angle of onset, natural oscillations of the eye may be mistaken for nystagmus.

3. Field Evaluation of a Behavioral Test Battery for DWI, September 1983

Title: *Field Evaluation of a Behavioral Test Battery for DWI*

Authors: Theodore E. Anderson, Robert M. Schweitz, and Monroe B. Snyder

Performing Organization: Office of Driver and Pedestrian Research, Problem-Behavior Research Division

Department of Transportation Number DOT HS 806 475

The first thing to realize about this study is that it was small, both in scope and length. The study itself took only three months to perform. Its objective was to evaluate the use of the 3-test battery crafted during the 1981 SCRI Study.

Police agencies from four jurisdictions were used (Arlington County, Virginia; Maryland State police; North Carolina State Police; and Washington, D.C. Police). The study lasted from November 15, 1982 through February 15, 1983. The Arlington County Police data was only two months instead of three. They had issues with the legality of the breath tests used in their jurisdiction.

There were major problems with the accuracy of the study. Although the officers were given a one-day training class as well as a manual, it was difficult for the researchers to actually monitor the police data-collection in the field. The study notes this issue:

> It was not possible for researchers to routinely accompany the patrols and supervise the actual data collection. Therefore, no statements can be made as to how closely the requested data collection procedures were followed.

In fact, the data relating to the frequency of the monitors riding along with the police is not mentioned in the study which leads one to believe that it was very, very low. Moreover, with the exception of the North Carolina State Police, all agencies equipped their officers with PBTs. Since the focus of the study was to determine the efficacy of the three-test battery, the presence and use of PBTs would certainly interfere with the officers' decisions as to arrest or not arrest. Don't forget—this was a study with real drivers, on real roadways, who could be charged with real crimes. If an officer stopped and tested someone with FSTs and determined that the driver was not impaired, yet used a PBT which showed a .150 BAC, that officer would have to arrest the driver. One could only imagine the possible liability incurred if the officer let the driver go and he or she killed someone. The converse is also true—imagine the scenario where the officer administers the "new" and unproven test battery, the driver fails all three tests, yet blows a .003 BAC on the PBT. Instead of releasing that individual, the officer arrests for the sake of the research results. The study acknowledges this flaw:

> There are a number of problems in using these data. We do not know how those given a PBT differ from or are representative of the rest. Perhaps most significant of all, except for North Carolina, all agencies had PBTs available, and in the great majority of the cases, PBT data were available to the officer for a driver before he was arrested. Thus most arrest decisions were based on PBT data, rather than just the test battery data.

As one can plainly see by reading the study—a whopping 97% of Washington, D.C. police used PBTs during the investigation. Moreover, all drivers were stopped for suspicion of DUI which adds in another factor not contemplated by the study. Clearly, driving behavior had something to do with the ultimate arrest/not arrest decision made by the police. Unlike the laboratory evaluation, the police decision to arrest was already affected, if not skewed *toward* arrest, by the fact that all subjects were already suspected of DUI before the officers even met the subjects.

The combined accuracy rate of all police agencies (83%) was not far off from the laboratory study (80%). Of the misclassifications, however, 16% of the drivers were incorrectly classified as having a BAC of .10% or more. That means that 197 drivers were falsely arrested.

4. A Colorado Validation Study of the Standardized Field Sobriety Test (SFST) Battery, November 1995, Colorado
Authors: Ellen Anderson and Marcelline Burns
Performing Organization: Southern California Research Institute
Department of Transportation Number: None

The Colorado Study is among the most detailed of the six major studies and had two major differences from the other five. First, Colorado's weather was of particular concern to the researchers. Although in the end the study concluded that weather did not affect any of the results in a meaningful fashion, the study does say, "In particular, note that controlled laboratory conditions are less variable and, therefore, may be less challenging than the highly varied conditions which officers routinely encounter in the field."

Secondly, the Colorado Study is based on a differing legal standard. Note that the correct/incorrect decision to arrest or release may be skewed as compared to the other studies by Colorado's two-tiered laws which allow arrests at 0.10% (DUI) and at 0.05% (DWAI). Thus, the correct/incorrect arrest/release matrix is based on a 0.05% standard, not on a 0.10% or a 0.08% standard.

The study looked at data from 234 investigations. Officers used only the 3-test battery and were not equipped with PBTs. Trained observers were only with the officers 41% of the time (125 investigations). The observers, however, were all associated with law enforcement in some capacity. In fact, some were sworn police officers and some of those were in a dual-role of observer and participant. This is hardly the detached, neutral observer that one would hope for in a scientific study. It is not surprising that "The errors by officers that they reported were relatively minor in nature."

Women made up 18% of the total sample group of 305 drivers, yet they were 38% of the incorrect releases and 25% of the incorrect arrests. These numbers are statistically very significant.

No allowances were made for instrument error in BAC analysis. In fact, no allowances were made for instrument error in any of the six major studies, but the Colorado Study is the only one of the six studies to admit it.

With respect to HGN, the study noted: "It is possible that lack of smooth pursuit and distinct nystagmus at maximum deviation occur at low BACs with some subjects, but not with others, or on some occasions, but not others."

The Colorado Study recorded but did not correct for many variables that the other five studies did not record. In particular, the Colorado Study recorded:

- Weather conditions
- Temperature
- Type of Roadway
- Roadway Conditions
- Conditions of the surface used for the SFSTs
- Reason for the stop
- Related circumstances (major recreational events, holidays, taverns, bars and restaurants nearby)
- Open containers in the vehicle
- Driver's clothing (whether it was adequate for weather conditions)
- Driver's footwear
- Observer (present/absent)
- BAC by PBT (Yes/No)
- If yes, Measured BAC

The Colorado Study, to its credit, published the most complete and varied list of factors which were noted throughout each investigation. Compare this with the San Diego Study which has not released its raw data for analysis.

The data-gathering took place between February 22, 1995 and July 30, 1995, yielding 305 records from six Colorado Law Enforcement Agencies. (Seven agencies initially participated, but one agency provided no data.)

The study notes in its conclusion, "The records collected and analyzed during this study provide evidence that the SFSTs, as used at roadside by trained and experienced law enforcement officers, are valid indices of the presence of alcohol." Since this study used an arrest/release decision matrix of 0.05%, it really tells us nothing about the effectiveness of the 3-test battery at BACs of 0.08% or 0.10% because a segment of the "correctly identified" arrestees were lower than 0.08%.

Overall, for 234 cases confirmed by chemical tests, the officers' decisions to arrest and release were 86% correct, and 93% of their arrest decisions were correct—keeping in mind that the correct/incorrect decision was based on a statutory limit of 0.05%.

ANALYSIS: THE SAN DIEGO STUDY

5. Validation of the Standardized Field Sobriety Test Battery at BACs Below .10 Percent, August 1998, San Diego.
Authors: Jack Stuster and Marcelline Burns
Performing Organization: ANACAPA Sciences, Inc.
Department of Transportation Number: DOT HS 808 839

Only seven officers from one agency in San Diego took part in this study. The results of the HGN were adjusted to assume that four of six cues indicated a BAC of .08 or more, as opposed to .10 or more and that two cues or more indicated a BAC of .04 or more. The study does not mention which of the six cues were noted for the correlation. Two or more cues on the Walk-and-Turn and the One-Leg-Stand were said to represent .08 or more. The study group was similarly small in scale at only 297 motorists who were ultimately examined and given breath tests. Just 12.1% of the motorists were females.

HGN was found to be the most effective of the three-test SFST battery used, and the addition of the Walk-and-Turn and the One-Leg-Stand to the HGN did not raise the probability of determining the BAC significantly. The study asked officers to determine whether a person's BAC was above .08 and if below .08, to estimate whether the person's BAC was above a .04. The study claims not only good correlation between SFSTs and the .08 limit, but also claims good correlation between SFSTs and a .04 level.

The officers were asked not only to estimate whether the motorist was over or under the aforementioned levels, but also to estimate an actual BAC. The mean estimation for the entire group was .117. The actual mean of the recorded BACs was .122. Being averages, this tells us nothing about the efficacy of the individual estimations made and provides only "fluff" for the police and prosecution witnesses to cast the study in a more favorable light.

The study claims a very suspect 91% accuracy rate at the .08 level and 94% for .04. The officers were advised not to use any other tests besides the SFST Battery for their initial determination of estimated BAC. Note that ALL officers were equipped with NHTSA approved portable breath testing devices. They were asked to confirm the BACs of all people who were examined and ultimately arrested or released so that the study could report the results of those people who had failed the SFST Battery, as well as those who passed it. The study claims to have avoided the problems of officers administering a breath test before recording their estimation of the BAC by requiring them to estimate the BAC before using the breath tester. There was little supervision. Project staff monitors "periodically" rode with participating officers.

There were 24 false positive cases. That means that 24 people were arrested who should have been let go. The researchers note that nine of the 24 were within the margin of error of the breath testing machine, clearly implying that those drivers might have actually been over the limit. Yet the study does not find it important enough to mention the number of motorists who were over the limit, but also fell within the margin of error. Moreover, the study notes that one of the false positives was a minor. Thus, it was a correct-arrest decision because California has a zero-tolerance law for those under 21. They also discount a false positive because, although she had a measured BAC of .05, she was a "psychiatric patient." It seems, even to the casual observer, that this study is slanted in favor of the police.

Officers were required to be formally trained and have significant DUI experience in order to be part of the study. The study says, "Only trained and experienced test administrators could be permitted to participate in the *current* study to avoid confounding study results with the effects of substantially different officer skill and experience levels in SFST administration and scoring." This statement clearly helps the defense community in the situation where an inexperienced officer made the arrest. In other words, the San Diego findings apply only to experienced officers, with an intimate knowledge of the SFSTs. If we look back to the earlier studies with untrained and inexperienced officers, those studies claim a much lower correlation percentage at a much higher BAC.

The study contains two important quotes for the defense, both found at page 28:

> Horizontal gaze nystagmus lacks face validity because it does not appear to be linked to the requirements of driving a motor vehicle. The reasoning is correct, but it is based on the incorrect assumption that field sobriety tests are designed to measure driving impairment.

and;

> It is unlikely that complex human performance, such as that required to safely drive an automobile, can be measured at roadside...The link between BAC and driving impairment is a separate issue, involving entirely different research methods.

6. Title: A Florida Validation Study of the Standardized Field Sobriety Test (S.F.S.T.) Battery

Authors: Marcelline Burns

Performing Organization: Institute of Police Technology and Management, University of North Florida, Pinellas County Sheriff's Office, Southern California Research Institute

Department of Transportation Number: None

Chronologically, this is the last of the six major studies. Although it was a small sample group of drivers, the study seems to have been done with many (but not all) clinical controls in place. For example, there were 379 drivers stopped, but only 256 were evaluated for the final report. This is because in 13 cases, SFSTs were not administered; in 53 cases other tests were used in addition to the 3-test battery (most often the Finger-to-Nose and the Romberg); and 57 drivers refused the breath test, leaving a paltry 256 drivers who were used in the study.

Supposedly none of the officers were equipped with PBTs, but observers were only present 63% of the time. In other words, 140 of the original 379 investigations were not observed. There is no breakdown as to the percentage of the final 256 investigations which went without observation. The study used only eight police officers and lasted from June 1, 1997 to September 4, 1997.

Nine people were incorrectly arrested and nine were incorrectly released. Those drivers who were released had no legal obligation to take a breath test, but took one anyway at the request of the observers. They were told that if they were over the limit, they would not be arrested unless they chose to drive away from the scene. Alternative transportation was provided. Four of the nine incorrectly arrested had BACs below 0.05%.

The study shows that failures to arrest alcohol impaired drivers included subjects who were able to perform the Walk-and-Turn and the One-Leg-Stand with little difficulty, but who displayed four or more cues on the HGN. The study opines that the incorrect release decisions may have been due to the officers being "misled" by the lack of psychomotor impairment.

The author of *this* book opines that the reason that the officers were "misled" is because not all people are impaired at levels of 0.08% and above.

2.8 Standardized Field Sobriety Test Battery

The Standardized Field Sobriety Test Battery (better known as SFSTs) is a series of three tests modified, standardized and validated for law enforcement use since the mid-1970s. It is important to realize that many of the SFSTs as well as the non-standardized FSTs have a real basis in the medical setting. HGN has been used for years to diagnose gross neurological dysfunction. The Walk-and-Turn test has been used by physicians and neurologists. The Romberg Sway test was used to assess patients in the tertiary stages of syphilis.

Because the tests have been used in the medical setting, it was thought that they may have application in the DUI setting. This is not entirely implausible. Alcohol intoxication is a neurological dysfunction and has certain symptoms which may be measured by physical tests. A brain tumor may also cause a neurological dysfunction with certain symptoms which may be measured by physical tests. This does not mean, however, that minimally trained police officers can accurately diagnose alcohol intoxication by the side of the road, in poor lighting, with a nervous subject, with no medical history, and with only crude tests. Yet this is exactly what they do on a daily basis.

The SFSTs are all, with two exceptions, divided attention tasks. That is, they require subjects to divide their attention between a mental task (remembering and following instructions) and a physical task (generally balancing). The two exceptions are Horizontal Gaze Nystagmus and Vertical Gaze Nystagmus which are not divided attention tasks, but merely show an involuntary muscle movement.

The SFSTs are not a measure of one's ability to drive. They merely correlate to a percentage chance that a person is at or above a specific BAC.

A. Horizontal Gaze Nystagmus (HGN)

Like all FSTs, HGN does not predict impairment, but actually correlates performance on the test with a percentage probability that the subject is at or above a particular BAC. HGN is the only part of the SFST three-test battery that is not a divided attention task.

In some states, officers must pass a police-taught course and show some level of proficiency in practical applications in order to administer the test and have it be admissible in court. Among the requirements by some police agencies is that an officer maintain an HGN Log wherein the officer records HGN exams, results, and a BAC. In this manner, one can tell whether the officer is maintaining his or her department-required proficiency level. In other states such as Kansas, HGN is entirely inadmissible in court.

The best strategy for HGN is the simplest strategy. Defense attorneys tend to get caught up in the minutia of HGN. There are subtle nuances involved with deciphering HGN that attorneys take for granted. The moment that you assume that a jury understands HGN, you have lost the HGN battle. In a nutshell, the jury should be made to understand the following message:

- HGN is a very scientific, complex examination.
- Under the proper circumstances, and with much education, competent medical personnel can use HGN as a diagnostic tool for measuring gross neurological dysfunction.
- The officer has neither the training nor the intelligence to properly administer or evaluate the HGN Exam, therefore the results are worthless.
- The circumstances under which the HGN was administered make the test results a virtual nullity.

It is important to realize that HGN is not a police-developed test. HGN is really a medical test used by doctors to diagnose head injuries and other pathological brain dysfunction. HGN only made its way into police use through NHTSA.

HGN Instructions

The instructions as given in *DWI Detection and Standardized Field Sobriety Testing*, Participant Manual, 2004 Edition (HS 178 R9/04Session VIII, "Concepts and Principles for the Standardized Field Sobriety Tests," are as follows:

> "If the suspect is wearing eyeglasses, have them removed.
>
> Give the suspect the following instructions from a safe position. (FOR OFFICER SAFETY KEEP YOUR WEAPON AWAY FROM THE SUSPECT):
>
> "I am going to check your eyes."
> "Keep your head still and follow the stimulus with your eyes only."
> "Keep following the stimulus with your eyes until I tell you to stop."
>
> "Position the stimulus approximately 12-15 inches from the suspect's nose and slightly above eye level. Check to see that both pupils are equal in size. If they are not, this may indicate a head injury. You may observe Resting Nystagmus at this time, then check the suspect's eyes for the ability to track together. Move the stimulus smoothly across the suspect's entire field of vision. Check to see if the eyes track the stimulus together or one lags behind the other. If the eyes don't track together, it could indicate a possible medical disorder, injury or blindness.

Check the suspect's left eye by moving the stimulus to your right. Move the stimulus smoothly, at a speed that requires approximately two seconds to bring the suspect's eye as far to the side as it can go. While moving the stimulus, look at the suspect's eye and determine whether it is able to pursue smoothly. Now, move the stimulus all the way to the left, back across the suspect's face checking if the right eye pursues smoothly. Movement of the stimulus should take approximately two seconds out and two seconds back for each eye. Repeat the procedure.

After you have checked both eyes for lack of smooth pursuit, check the eyes for distinct and sustained nystagmus at maximum deviation beginning with the suspect's left eye. Simply move the object to the suspect's left side until the eye has gone as far to the side as possible. Usually, no white will be showing in the corner of the eye at maximum deviation. Hold the eye at that position for a minimum of four seconds, and observe the eye for distinct and sustained nystagmus. Move the stimulus all the way across the suspect's face to check the right eye holding that position for a minimum of four seconds."

"Next, check for onset of nystagmus prior to 45 degrees. Start moving the stimulus towards the right (suspect's left eye) at a speed that would take approximately four seconds for the stimulus to reach the edge of the suspect's shoulder. Watch the eye carefully for any sign of jerking. When you see it, stop and verify that the jerking continues. Now, move the stimulus to the left (suspect's right eye) at a speed that would take approximately four seconds to reach the edge of the suspect's shoulder. Watch the eye carefully for any sign of jerking. When you see it, stop and verify that the jerking continues. Repeat the procedure. NOTE: It is important to use the full four seconds when checking for onset of nystagmus. If you move the stimulus too fast, you may go past the point of onset or miss it altogether."

"If the suspect's eyes start jerking before they reach 45 degrees, check to see that some white of the eye is still showing on the side closest to the ear. If no white of the eye is showing, you either have taken the eye too far to the side, (that is more than 45 degrees) or the person has unusual eyes that will not deviate very far to the side."

"NOTE: Nystagmus may be due to causes other than alcohol. These other causes include seizure medications and some other drugs. A large disparity between the performance of the right eye and the left eye may indicate a medical condition."

Test Interpretation

You should look for three clues of nystagmus in each eye.

1. The eye cannot follow a moving object smoothly.

2. Nystagmus is distinct and sustained when the eye is held at maximum deviation for a minimum of four seconds.

3. The angle of onset of nystagmus is prior to 45 degrees."

Although there have been newer studies which correlate HGN to a percentage chance that the subject is .08 or more, the 2004 NHTSA SFST manual still refers the student to the original studies conducted in the 1970s and 1980s which correlate 6 out of 6 cues with a 77% chance that the subject is .10 or higher.

B. Walk-and-Turn

The Walk-and-Turn (WAT) test is a divided attention task that requires a subject to listen to and follow instructions as given and demonstrated by the officer. Generally, it requires the subject to stand in a heel-to-toe fashion for a period of time, then to walk heel-to-toe nine steps down a straight line, turn at the ninth step in the manner demonstrated and walk back nine steps in the same fashion.

The instructions as given in *DWI Detection and Standardized Field Sobriety Testing*, Participant Manual, 2004 Edition (HS 178 R9/04Session VIII, "Concepts and Principles for the Standardized Field Sobriety Tests") are as follows:

"1. Instructions Stage: Initial Positioning and Verbal Instructions

For standardization in the performance of this test, have the suspect assume the heel-to-toe stance by giving the following verbal instructions, accompanied by demonstrations:

"Place your left foot on the line" (real or imaginary). Demonstrate.

"Place your right foot on the line ahead of the left foot, with the heel of right foot against toe of left foot." Demonstrate.

"Place your arms down by your sides." Demonstrate.

"Maintain this position until I have completed the instructions. Do not start to walk until told to do so."

"Do you understand the instructions so far?" (Make sure the suspect indicates understanding."

"2. Demonstrations and Instructions for the Walking Stage.
Explain the test requirements, using the following verbal instruction, accompanied by demonstrations:

"When I tell you to start, take nine heel-to-toe steps, turn, and take nine heel-to-toe steps back." (Demonstrate 3 heel-to-toe steps).

"When you turn, keep the front foot on the line, and turn by taking a series of small steps with the other foot, like this." (Demonstrate).

"While you are walking, keep your arms at your sides, watch your feet at all times, and count your steps out loud."

"Once you start walking, don't stop until you have completed the test."

"Do you understand the instructions?" (make sure the suspect understands).

"Begin, and count your first step from the heel-to-toe position as 'One'".

"3. Test Interpretation
You may observe a number of different behaviors when a suspect performs this test. Original research demonstrated the behaviors listed below are likely to be observed in someone with a BAC above 0.10. Look for the following clues each time this test is given:

A. Cannot keep balance while listening to instructions. Two tasks are required at the beginning of this test. The suspect must balance heel-to-toe on the line, and at the same time, listen carefully to the instructions. Typically, the person who is impaired can do only one of these things. The suspect may listen to the instructions, but not keep balance. Record this clue if the suspect does not maintain the heel-to-toe position throughout the instructions. (Feet must actually break apart.) Do not record this clue if the suspect sways or uses arms to balance but maintains the heel-to-toe position.

B. Starts before the instructions are finished. The impaired person may also keep balance, but not listen to the instructions. Since you specifically instructed the suspect not to start walking "until I tell you to begin," record the clue if the suspect does not wait.

C. Stops while walking. The suspect pauses for several seconds. Do not record this clue if the suspect is merely walking slowly.

D. Does not touch heel-to-toe. The suspect leaves a space of more than one-half inch between the heel and toe on any step.

E. Steps off the line. The suspect steps so that one foot is entirely off the line.

F. Uses arms to balance. The suspect raises one or both arms more than 6 inches from the sides in order to maintain balance.

G. Improper turn. The suspect removes the front foot from the line while turning. Also record this clue if the suspect has not followed directions as demonstrated, i.e., spins or pivots around.

H. Incorrect number of steps. Record this clue if the suspect takes more or fewer than nine steps in either direction."

"Note: If suspect can't do the test, record observed clues and document the reason for not completing the test, e.g. suspect's safety.

If the suspect has difficulty with the test (for example, steps off the line), continue from that point, not from the beginning. This test may also lose its sensitivity if it is repeated several times.

Observe the suspect from a safe distance and limit your movement which may distract the suspect during the test. **Always consider officer safety.**

Based on the original research, if the suspect exhibits two or more clues on this test or fails to complete it, classify the suspect's BAC as above 0.10. Using this criterion, you will be able to accurately classify 68% of your suspects."

"Test Conditions

Walk-and-Turn test requires a designated straight line, and should be conducted on a reasonably dry, hard, level, nonslippery surface. There should be sufficient room for suspects to complete nine heel-to-toe steps. Note: Recent field validation studies have indicated that varying environmental conditions have not affected a suspect's ability to perform this test.

The original research indicated that individuals over 65 years of age, back, leg or middle ear problems had difficulty performing this test. Individuals wearing heels more than 2 inches high should be given the opportunity to remove their shoes."

C. One Leg Stand

The One Leg Stand (OLS) test is a divided attention task that requires a subject to listen to and follow instructions as given and demonstrated by the officer. Generally, it requires the subject to stand on one leg, arms at the subject's side, while the subject watches his raised foot and counts out loud for 30 seconds.

The instructions as given in *DWI Detection and Standardized Field Sobriety Testing*, Participant Manual, 2004 Edition (HS 178 R9/04Session VIII, "Concepts and Principles for the Standardized Field Sobriety Tests") are as follows:

"1. Instructions Stage: Initial Positioning and Verbal Instructions
Initiate the test by giving the following verbal instructions, accompanied by demonstrations.

"Please stand with your feet together and your arms down at the sides, like this." (Demonstrate).

"Do not start to perform the test until I tell you to do so."

"Do you understand the instructions so far"? (Make sure suspect indicates understanding).

2. Demonstrations and Instructions for the Balance and Counting Stage
Explain the test requirements, using the following verbal instructions, accompanied by demonstrations.

"When I tell you to start, raise one leg, either leg, with the foot approximately 6 inches off the ground, keeping your raised foot parallel to the ground." (Demonstrate one leg stance.)

"You must keep both legs straight, arms at your side."

"While holding this position, count out loud in the following manner: "one thousand and one, one thousand and two, one thousand and three, until told to stop." (Demonstrate and count, as follows: "one thousand and one, one thousand and two, one thousand and three, etc." Officer should not look at his foot when conducting the demonstration —OFFICER SAFETY.)

"Keep your arms at your sides at all times and keep watching the raised foot."

"Do you understand?" (Make sure the suspect indicates understanding.)

"Go ahead and perform the test." (Officer should always time the 30 seconds. Test should be discontinued after 30 seconds).

Observe the suspect from a safe distance. If the suspect puts the foot down, give instructions to pick the foot up again and continue counting from the point at which the foot touched the ground. If the suspect counts very slowly, terminate the test after 30 seconds.

3. Test Interpretation

You may observe a number of different behaviors when a suspect performs this test. The original research found the behaviors listed below are the most likely to be observed in someone with a BAC above 0.10. Look for the following clues each time the One-Leg-Stand test is administered.

A. The suspect sways while balancing. This refers to side-to-side or back-and-forth motion while the suspect maintains the one-leg stand position.

B. Uses arms for balance. Suspect moves arms 6 or more inches from the side of the body in order to keep balance.

C. Hopping. Suspect is able to keep one foot off the ground, but resorts to hopping to maintain balance.

D. Puts foot down. The suspect is not able to maintain the one-leg stand position, putting foot down one or more times during the 30-second count.

Note: If suspect can't do the test, record observed clues and document the reason for not completing the test, e.g. suspect's safety.

Remember that time is critical in this test. The original research has shown that a person with a BAC above 0.10 can maintain balance for up to 25 seconds, but seldom as long as 30.

Based on original research, if an individual displays two or more clues or fails to complete the One-Leg Stand, there is a good chance the BAC is above 0.10. Using that criterion, you will accurately classify 65% of the people you test as to whether their BAC's are above 0.10.

Observe the suspect from a safe distance and remain as motionless as possible during the test so as not to interfere. If the suspect puts the foot down, give instructions to pick the foot up again and continue counting from the point at which the foot touched the ground. If the suspect counts very slowly, terminate the test after 30 seconds.

4. Test Conditions

One-Leg Stand requires a reasonable dry, hard, level, and non-slippery surface. Suspect's safety should be considered at all times. The original research indicated that certain individuals over 65 years of age, back, leg or middle ear problems, or people who are overweight by 50 or more pounds had difficulty performing this test. Individuals wearing heels more than 2 inches high should be given the opportunity to remove their shoes.

2.9 Commonly Used Non-Standardized/Validated Field Sobriety Tests

Non-Standardized and Non-Validated FSTs provide wonderful fodder for cross-examination. Where the strategy is appropriate to your overall defense, these tests may allow your attorney to use the "Damned-if-you-do, Damned-if-you-don't" principle. If the officer used the tests and you passed them, they may be built up as the best predictors of intoxication known to man. Clearly there is no statistical evidence that shows that the Non-Standardized/Non-Validated FSTs have any value, but the common-sense argument would be to ask how someone who is so unsafe to drive, could touch the tip of his finger to the tip of his nose, while his eyes are closed, by the side of the road. If the officer starts to discount the efficacy of the test, he can be hammered with the fact that his police agency certainly would not administer bogus tests to the public. In fact, had you "failed" the test, that fact would be used against you without mercy.

If, on the other hand, you failed the test, your attorney can attack the officer on grounds of lack of research to back the tests. Clearly, your attorney will want to stay away from the subject of correlation to BAC, but he or she can use the prosecutor's trick of asking if the tests are Standardized and Validated. Your attorney can ask if they are used by the police all over the country. Your attorney can ask if they are used and evaluated the same way, every time by different officers. Finally, your attorney can ask if they are "approved" for use on human beings by the National Highway Traffic Safety Administration.

As with all advice in this book, the above is simply an illustration of what may be logically argued on your behalf by your attorney. It is not a substitute for your attorney's advice, skill, education and style. Local rules, case law, statute and strategy may predict a different course for cross-examination.

A. Vertical Gaze Nystagmus (VGN)

Vertical Gaze Nystagmus is taught to police officers as part of their HGN training. VGN is a jerking movement of the eyes in the vertical (up/down) plane as the subject follows a stimulus that is moved from about eye-level to well above the subject's head. The subject's head remains still as the subject follows the stimulus using his or her eyes, only.

Unlike HGN, the police are taught that VGN does not correlate to any particular BAC. Rather they are told that VGN indicates a particularly high BAC for that subject. Obviously, this leads to some serious questions of validity. First and foremost, one would have to determine what "a particularly high BAC" would be for the subject in question.

Moreover, there is a relevance problem involved. Even if the basic premise of VGN were correct, of what relevance would such evidence be to a jury? Suppose a .03 is a particularly high BAC for the individual. VGN would neither suggest that the person is over the limit of .08, nor suggest intoxication. It would simply show that the subject does not normally have a BAC of .03.

Suppose .315 is a particularly high BAC for the individual. VGN would neither suggest that the person is over the limit of .08 (no correlation), nor that the person is intoxicated. It adds nothing to the elements that must be proved by the prosecution.

B. Romberg Modified

Part of the original studies, the Romberg Test was also researched in the later NHTSA-funded studies. The Romberg (commonly misspelled as "Rhomberg") test is a real, medical test used by neurologists throughout the world. It was first developed by Dr. Moritz Romberg in the mid-1800s and the sway was called "Romberg Sign" which is short for a sign of static ataxia in the tabes dorsalis (in laymen's terms, it is a measure of postural control in darkness). Ironically, he taught a well-attended "propaedeutic clinic" which used practical demonstrations to emphasize the importance of careful medical examinations which would ensure a correct diagnosis. Dr. Romberg would likely be shocked to find that his test is used at the roadside by minimally trained officers to diagnose alcohol impairment.

To perform the test, the person is instructed to stand with feet together, head tipped back, eyes closed, and arms down at the sides. An anterior-posterior sway is noted. The test lasts for 45 seconds.

There is nothing noted in Dr. Romberg's description of the test to suggest that the head be tipped back as required by the police. Moreover, there is no time-limit to his test. The results of the Romberg Test could as easily diagnose alcohol impairment as it could diagnose a person in the tertiary stages of syphilis.

C. Finger-to-Nose

The instructions are that the subject stands erect with eyes closed and arms extended horizontally. The subject is then instructed to touch the nose with the index finger, alternating right and left hands as instructed. A demonstration is given by the officer.

The instructions above are from the original research into the efficacy of the FSTs. There have been no rewrites of the instructions, or official modifications to the instructions. Watch for officers asking that the person touch the "tip" of their finger to the "tip" of their noses and then counting the subject off for using the pad of the finger. Notice that the instructions say nothing about the "tip" of either the finger or the nose. The instructions simply ask the person to "touch the nose with the index finger." This could presumably mean that one could touch the bridge of the nose with any part of the index finger.

D. Finger Count

Also one of the original FSTs considered for use in the 3-Test Battery, the Finger Count was rejected for use. The instructions are that the subject must touch and count each finger in succession, using the thumb, while counting aloud. The test is demonstrated as "Watch what I do. 1-2-3-4-5-5-4-3-2-1."

The Finger Count is probably one of the most difficult tests to perform, although it sounds like it would be the easiest to perform. Some people simply do not have good manual dexterity, but the more likely reason (unsupported by research) is that the test is extremely sensitive to alcohol.

Chapter 3

Chemical Testing

3.1 Chapter Overview

This chapter deals with breath and blood testing. It covers the basics of breath testing with three common methods of attacks. Be wary, however, that not all attacks will be relevant to your case. Moreover, many states have eliminated certain types of attacks on breath testing. This means that there may be certain errors and variances that actually made your breath test inaccurate, but your attorney will not be allowed to present those facts to a jury.

Blood testing covers the entire process from the vein to the forensic crime lab. Blood kits, phlebotomy, and headspace gas chromatography are discussed. Keep in mind that the forensic blood testing process is far different than most hospital blood testing procedures.

3.2 Breath Testing Basics

A. Evidential Breath Testing

An Evidential Breath Test is intended to be admissible in court. However, this does not mean that a non-evidential breath test will not be admitted. The term "evidential breath test" refers to the intended use, not its actual use. Evidential breath testers (EBT) use one of two technologies: Infrared Light Absorption or Fuel Cell technology. Infrared is far more commonly used in the United States and has a much longer history than fuel cells. Each has its advantages and disadvantages.

Infrared is not specific to the alcohol molecule. It can mistake many other compounds for ethanol. Yet within certain limitations, it is far better than a fuel cell device for quantification. Fuel cell devices are far more specific for ethanol, but have significant issues when it comes to quantifying a result. Infrared EBTs are generally heavier and far less portable than fuel cell devices. Fuel cell EBTs are, generally, hand-held and can be battery-powered.

B. Infrared Light Absorption

All the Infrared EBTs use infrared light (IR) absorption to detect alcohol. Both visible and IR light are wavelengths of what is known as the electromagnetic spectrum. Humans and animals can see visible light (hence the name, "visible light"). Other wavelengths of the electromagnetic spectrum are invisible to us, such as radio waves. The wavelengths in the spectrum vary in size from the height of skyscrapers to very short gamma rays, smaller than the nucleus of an atom. IR light is invisible to the human eye.

Electromagnetic wavelengths are measured in terms of microns (one-millionth of a meter). The wavelength of the light that we see is from 0.4 microns (blue light) to 0.7 microns (red light).

The Electromagnetic Spectrum

Portion of the Spectrum	Wavelength in Microns
Radio Waves	Greater than 10^{+3}
Microwaves	25 to 10^{+3}
Far Infrared	15 to 50
Mid Infrared	2.5 to 15
Near Infrared	0.7 to 2.5
Visible Light	0.4 (blue) to 0.7 (red)
Ultraviolet	10^{-3} to 4×10^{-1}
X-rays	10^{-6} to 10^{-3}
Gamma Rays	Less than 10^{-6}

Organic molecules are made up of groups of atoms. IR light is absorbed by organic molecules, in this case ethanol, and converted into a type of energy called "molecular vibration." Certain groups of those atoms will absorb bands of IR light at or near predictable and characteristic wavelengths irrespective of the structure of the rest of the organic molecule. Alcohol is one of those molecules. Since alcohol molecules have characteristic wavelengths of absorption, the EBTs are set to filter IR light at those particular wavelengths and measure it. Different EBTs use different filters. Alcohol will generally absorb IR light at or near 3.4–3.5 microns and at or near 9.4 microns.

Structure of the EtOH Molecule

H = Hydrogen Atom
C = Carbon Atom
O = Oxygen Atom

```
  H   H
   \ /
H— C-C-O-H
   / \
  H   H
```

Chemical Subgroups of Atoms of the EtOH Molecule

```
              Methylene Group CH2
   H            H
    \          /
H—C           -C-          -O-H
   /            \        Hydroxy or
  H             H        Alcohol Group OH
Methyl Group CH3
```

Most devices measure the C-H bonds (3.38 to 3.48 microns) of the methyl group and of the similar C-H bonds of the methylene group (3.43 to 3.51 microns), while a few devices measure the C-O (7.93 to 10.00 microns) of the alcohol group.

C. Basic Operation of an Infrared Breath Tester

Most people think of the breath test reading a percentage of alcohol in the blood. This is incorrect. Breath testing attempts to measure the amount of alcohol in the breath, which is then used to estimate the amount of alcohol in the blood. All law enforcement breath test results in the United States are expressed as weight per volume in units of grams of alcohol per 210 liters of breath (about 55 gallons).

The basic operation of Infrared Breath Testing machines is that IR light is shined through a sample chamber tube. The amount of light that passes through the tube is captured at the other end of the tube by a detector. The light energy captured is then converted to an electrical signal correlating to a baseline according to the software programmed into the machine.

When a person blows into the machine, the alcohol molecules that are in the breath absorb some of the IR light as it passes through the sample chamber tube. This means that less IR light strikes the detector than before the breath entered the sample chamber tube. The machine's software calculates the difference in the amount of IR light detected before the person blew (baseline) and while the breath was in the sample chamber tube (second reading) and converts this to a BAC that is printed in conformance with the Uniform Vehicle Code of grams of alcohol per 210 liters of breath.

Because different molecules absorb light of different wavelengths, and because the wavelengths at which alcohol absorbs IR light are well-known, the machines all use IR filters that allow only certain wavelengths of IR light to pass through, corresponding to the wavelengths that the alcohol molecules absorb. If they did not filter the light, then theoretically one could blow smoke through the sample chamber, reducing all wavelengths of light and get a positive reading for alcohol. This problem is avoided by several means, both internal and external to the machine.

Most machines have some sort of reference IR filter in addition to the filters meant for alcohol and other substances. The reference filter is set at a wavelength that nothing on the human breath should interfere with. If the machine detects a drop in the light shone through the tube at the reference wavelength, or if it is not captured by the IR detector at the proper time, then the machine should abort the test.

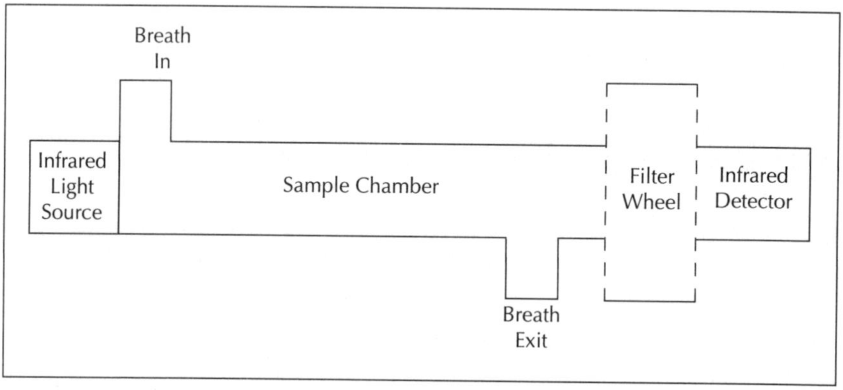

Sample Infrared Diagram

D. Breath Testing: Methods of Attack

There are three areas of attack on any breath test: machine based, operator based, and subject based.

1. Machine-based attacks

a. Intermittent problems

Intermittent problems include vibrations to the machine while it is working, inadequate or improper power supplies, filter-wheel motors and fluctuating baselines. Some machines are used in the backs of patrol cars or inside vans. In addition to the inherent vibration associated with a running engine, power supplies can fluctuate as well. Watch for calibration logs from these mobile machines.

Often, they are removed from the vehicle and tested inside a building with a stable power source. Unstable power sources can result in a fluctuating baseline reading, inconsistent rpm on the filter-wheel motor, dimming or brightening IR source lamps and other problems. Your state's breath testing regulations may require a dedicated power source.

b. Warranty

Most breath testers are not warranted to test breath for alcohol accurately or reliably by the manufacturer. This can be brought out at trial with an Expert Witness and the machine's manual. Most juries don't like the fact that the manufacturer of the machine doesn't even warrant that it will test breath accurately.

c. Lack of concurrent calibration checks

A concurrent calibration check means that the machine does a calibration check with a known standard alcohol solution (either dry-gas or a wet-bath simulator) immediately prior to and after the subject test. This provides a calibration check within minutes before and minutes after a subject test. It is considered to be the most reliable method of calibration checks on a breath tester. Anything else is substandard in the eyes of the forensic toxicology community.

d. Computer Database Records

Most state of the art breath testers produced today have computer data storage and communications capabilities. Generally, they can record everything that happens with the machine. Most are capable of recording subject tests, quality assurance testing, error codes and more. The data can certainly be used to check the trends of individual machines for machine-based errors, but they can also be used to track officers for operator-based errors. (See Operator-Based Attacks, below.)

The lack of such data is certainly worthy of an attack in virtually every DUI case. Simply put, more data points are better than less data when one is asked to review quality assurance records of a machine. Certainly one can review monthly, hand-written calibration checks to determine whether a particular machine was working properly or not on any date in between those checks, but one has to assume no maintenance or repairs during that time frame as well. Computer data can provide much of that missing information for a reviewing forensic toxicologist. With software and downloading capabilities readily available, there is no valid reason for any agency not to use a manufacturer's data package.

e. Inherent margin of error

Many state codes require that all breath testing machines be capable of achieving a result to within ±10% of the known standard used, or within .01 BAC, whichever is greater. Some states allow smaller margins of error. This is because all measuring devices have some error. Some devices may have greater accuracy or precision than others, but they all encompass some error. The accuracy rate is based on a bell curve with standard deviations and statistically breaks down as follows:

680 out of 1,000 tests will be within 3.33%
950 out of 1,000 tests will be within 6.66%
997 out of 1,000 tests will be within 10%

This means that three out of 1,000 tests will fall outside of the required ±10%, but more importantly, it shows that the inherent margin of error is random. It can strike at any time, and there is no way to tell if it affected your test. If it is the state's burden to show that a defendant's test was over the legal limit by proof beyond every reasonable doubt, and if they cannot account for the ±10% inherent margin of error of a .085% result, then they cannot prove their case.

f. Radio Frequency Interference (RFI)

Probably the most overlooked and improperly used attack is RFI. RFI is an electromagnetic wave. We think of it most frequently as a police radio transmitting near a breath tester during the administration of a test. But that is not the most frequent source of RFI during a subject test. RFI is generated whenever and wherever an electric motor is running. Many breath testers have an electric motor turning the filter wheel, known as a "chopper motor." Many machines also have an RFI antenna as well as a heavy-duty metal case designed to shield the internal components from RFI. Both safeguards do a pretty good job, but herein lies the problem: the heavy-duty metal case shields the RFI antenna from *internal* RFI. Internal RFI exists every time the machine samples breath, and the externally located antenna will not pick it up. Experienced practitioners have all seen what we commonly refer to as "sick machines," i.e., those machines that seem to have a high number of inexplicable errors. Clearly, this problem could be caused by the inherent design flaw of the machine. Some new machines reduce the chances of this happening because they have no chopper motor.

g. Single-Test Errors

It is hard to believe, but some states still use a single-test instead of replicate testing. Note that some states only require a 15-minute deprivation period and samples that are far closer together than 15 minutes. Additionally, some states allow as much as a .03 difference between samples. The important thing to note is that each state has its own regulations. If the breath test is a single sample, many errors including mouth-alcohol are a serious concern.

2. Operator-based attacks

a. Inadequate deprivation period

Operators must ensure that the test subject has not ingested any alcoholic beverages or other fluids, vomited, eaten, smoked, burped or placed any foreign object in the mouth for at least 20 minutes immediately preceding the first sample, although some states require only 15 minutes.

b. Forced agreement

Forced agreement occurs where the breath test operator interrupts the subject's breathing pattern on the second of the two samples. The operator is supposed to tell the subject to take a deep breath and immediately blow all of that breath into the machine without stopping. The idea is to let the machine decide when an adequate sample has been taken. Once the machine determines that an adequate sample has been taken (by analyzing the profile of the slope of the alcohol curve), it will analyze the sample.

Savvy operators have realized that sometimes a second sample will not agree within .02 of the first sample by watching the digital display rising on the digital screen of the machine. This means that the operator will have to collect a third breath sample. Not only is this time-consuming in that it will not allow the officer to move on to the next DUI, but it will create an argument for the defense regarding mouth-alcohol. (See Subject-Based Attacks, below.)

When the operator sees the subject's second breath reading approach the level of the first breath reading, the operator will tell the subject to stop blowing or even pull the breath hose away from the subject's mouth. Often, the profile of the slope will be adequate for the machine to accept the reading, but had the subject blown longer, the second reading may have exceeded the first reading by more than .02. This is why it is important to tell your attorney if the officer told you when to start and stop blowing.

c. Breath holding—the longer you blow, the higher it goes

Operators are supposed to instruct subjects to take a deep breath and then immediately blow all of their breath into the machine. For officer safety, the police officers are instructed to hold the breath tube while the subject is blowing and not let the subject handle the breath hose. This is because some subjects have been known to grab a machine by the hose and swing it around, injuring the officer.

This instruction to the officer about holding the breath hose has led to both intentional and unintentional breath holding. An officer who wishes to make the breath test result higher may ask the subject to take a deep breath and then blow it into the machine as directed. The subject then takes a deep breath, but the officer does not immediately present the breath hose to the subject. Instead, the officer will hold onto the breath hose for a few moments while the subject is holding his or her breath.

3. Subject-based attacks

a. Breathing patterns

Hyperventilation and hypoventilation will cause as much as a ±15% variation in a breath test result. The longer a person holds his or her breath, the higher the result. Short, rapid breaths tend to flush out the lungs and result in a lower reading. This variance is most often seen when an operator has a subject hold his breath and then delays giving him the breath tube and when a subject is upset to the point of crying or nearly crying. People who are crying generally are not breathing in a normal pattern—which is required for accurate breath testing. The crying subject may take deep breaths and hold them or may also have short, shallow, rapid breathing. In any event, a crying subject is likely not breathing as expected for an evidential breath test.

b. Temperature

Temperature variations in the human body can change the amount of alcohol that is transferred from the blood to the breath. The amount of alcohol that passes from the blood into the breath is governed by *Henry's Law of Partial Pressures*, which is the cornerstone of forensic breath testing.

The concept is simple. The hotter a liquid, the more molecules of that liquid will pass into the gaseous phase. Take, for example, a small room with a very cold cup of black coffee sitting on a table in that room. It is likely that you would not smell the coffee unless you put your nose right at the lip of the cup. Take the same example, but substitute a steaming cup of coffee. Within minutes, the room would be filled with the coffee's aroma. This is because more molecules of the hot coffee passed into the gaseous phase and filled the room.

All machines expect a breath temperature of 34°C, but what they most often get is a breath temperature of 35°C. Each degree centigrade of variance equates to 8.6% variance in the breath test result. Thus, someone with a .075 BAC will test at a .081 BAC if breath temperature is 35°C. The IACT (International Association of Chemical Testers) Newsletter, Volume 9, Number 2, July 1998 carries an article by Dr. Dale Carpenter, Ph.D., and Dr. James A. Buttram, Ph.D., which shows that while 34°C is the accepted breath temperature for breath testing the human range starts at 32.4°C and rises to 36.2°C, with the average being 34.9°C. The argument is, if you are the average human being, your breath temperature is 1°C higher than what the machine is programmed to expect. Thus, your breath test result is 8.6% too high. Be sure to tell your attorney if there were any events which would lead to an even higher temperature due to illness, infection or menstrual cycles.

c. Hematocrit

Hematocrit is a number expressing the size and number of red blood cells in proportion to the rest of the blood. Hematocrit ratios vary in healthy human beings from 40.7% to 50% in men, and 36.1% to 44.3% in women. It can vary with altitude, illness, and state of hydration. The hematocrit level governs how much alcohol may be contained by the blood and, in turn, how much will pass into the breath. Normal hematocrit ratios will lead to a ±5% difference in a breath test result. Some experimental data shows up to a 14% variation.

d. Abnormal lung physiology

All breath testing machines are designed to test breath from average, healthy humans. When you have abnormal lung physiology, let your attorney know. Abnormal lung physiology could have three possible outcomes: raising the reported BAC, lowering the reported BAC or no effect on the reported BAC. Sometimes, you will not know what the result might be of certain types of abnormal lung physiology—it might make the BAC higher or lower—but isn't that the essence of reasonable doubt?

e. Mouth alcohol

Mouth alcohol is residual alcohol that remains in the mouth after drinking, or is introduced into the mouth via regurgitation, burping or any event which can bring stomach contents back up into the mouth and/or throat. In either event, mouth alcohol can add to a breath test result, increasing the value. All infrared machines have "slope detectors," sometimes called "mouth alcohol detectors." The slope detector is a software program that looks at the slope of the graph of the ethanol in breath profile. If the slope does not fall within the parameters of the slope programmed into the machine, the software is supposed to flag it as mouth alcohol, alert the operator and abort the test. The operator must conduct a new deprivation period before the next test. The three main parameters that must be followed to assure the operator of a valid test, free from the influence of mouth alcohol, are:

1. A valid 20-minute deprivation period

2. A working slope detector
3. Sample agreement within .02 and 15 to 20 minutes apart.

If any one of these three parameters is not met, scientific confidence in the validity of the results is lessened, and the test results may be inadmissible. The quality assurance records should reflect a tested and working slope detector, and the breath test cards should reflect sample agreement of no more than .02 apart and consecutive tests within 15 to 20 minutes of each other.

f. Partition ratio

In courtrooms that still allow the truth to be told to juries, partition ratio can be a very powerful argument. All breath testing machines in the United States are set to a partition ratio of 2100:1. In other words, for every one part of alcohol in a subject's breath, the machine is programmed to assume that there are another 2,100 parts in the blood. Thus, the machines perform a mathematical calculation to convert a breath alcohol concentration to a blood alcohol concentration and display the results in grams of alcohol per 210 liters of blood. This would be fine if all human beings had a constant partition ratio of 2100:1. We do not. The normal, healthy human body varies from 900:1 to about 3400:1.

3.3 Preliminary Breath Testing

Preliminary Breath Tests (PBT) are often used for probable cause purposes. Because they carry neither the safeguards nor the documentation of evidential breath testers, they are rarely admitted as evidence (California is the one of the notable exceptions to this and calls it the "Preliminary Alcohol Screening" (PAS)). Sometimes the prosecutor will attempt to admit the results to show "presence of alcohol" but with no quantification. If you acknowledged drinking, there is no real danger in admitting the result to show presence of alcohol only. The real danger, however, is when the courts are lulled into a sense of routine admission where the next step is to allow the prosecutor to admit the quantitative results. While this may or may not violate several rules of admissibility, it certainly violates the cornerstone principles of reliability of a breath test result.

A. Safeguards

Unless an evidential breath testing device is used for the PBT, there may be no safeguards against mouth alcohol. Even where an evidential machine is used, the other safeguards of replicate testing and a deprivation period will not be used. Thus, mouth alcohol can certainly be a factor.

Often, a PBT device will not be checked for function and accuracy by a quality assurance specialist, if it is tested at all. Maintenance logs and repair records are rarely kept for PBTs.

Unless an evidential breath testing machine is used as a PBT, radio frequency interference (RFI) may be present and interfere with the test, unknown to the officer.

3.4 Blood Testing Basics

If your case involves a blood test, review the following sections to determine if any of these issues were present in your case. Being arrested for a DUI is certainly a stressful situation and the fact that the government forces you to submit to a blood draw does not make it any less stressful, but the more that you can remember and communicate to your attorney gives you the best chance of beating the DUI.

The following issues may or may not have been present during your blood draw. It is important to review this section in its entirety to see if any of the issues were present.

A. Who May Draw Blood?

Virtually every state has rules and regulations regarding who may draw blood and under what circumstances. However, that does not mean that the courts will suppress a blood test result because the wrong person drew it. In fact, most states have said that when an unauthorized person draws blood, that fact will go to the weight that a jury gives to the result, not to the admissibility of the result.

A very disturbing trend has begun in my home state of Arizona, however, and it has recently spread beyond Arizona's borders. Police are now drawing blood on the scene. In Arizona, it has become common practice for the arresting officer, or another officer called to the scene, to produce a blood kit and draw blood from the suspect. Sometimes, the suspect is forced to stand, unsupported, while blood is being drawn. Not only do the police hurt people while doing this, they often contaminate the sample. Tell your attorney about the conditions under which your blood was drawn.

B. The Forensic Blood Kit

Police most often use a "blood kit" for law enforcement draws, although some jurisdictions simply allow hospital personnel to choose the components. It is important to note where the blood kit came from. Did you see it being taken from a closet in an emergency room at a hospital, or did the cop take it from the trunk of his car? Storage of the blood kit can have an effect on the integrity of the kit.

The expiration date of the tubes should always be checked. The preservative and anti-coagulant do not lose potency after expiration, but the seal on the tube is not guaranteed. This means that room air could leak into the tube through a compromised seal, bringing with it Candida Albicans or other contaminants. The antiseptic swab also has an expiration date crimped into the bottom edge of its foil wrapper. The tubes should be grey-topped, 10-ml. tubes. BD Vacutainer® is a brand of vacuum tubes made by Becton, Dickinson and Company (BD) and is the most common type found in blood kits. Other tube manufacturers are Lynn-Peavey, Tri-Tech and Monoject.

The grey top of the tube indicates a preservative and an anti-coagulant have been added to the tube. Grey-top tubes are used in the medical world for glucose testing procedures and were not developed strictly for law enforcement purposes. Be aware that the amount of preservative and anti-coagulant is a fixed volume and may differ from tube-to-tube. Some tubes are designed to yield a 1% strength preservative solution while others yield a 2% strength solution. This is important to note because two strains of bacteria have been found to produce alcohol in a 1% strength solution.

The preservative (or "antiglycolytic" agent) in a grey-top tube is sodium fluoride (chemical symbol: Na_2). The anticoagulant will be either EDTA (potassium edetate) or potassium oxalate. Potassium oxalate is more harsh on the red blood cells and can cause them to break apart more easily if the tubes are roughly handled. Other types of tubes are sometimes used when a forensic kit is unavailable. These must be scrutinized carefully for their chemical contents. As if the differing color tops wasn't confusing enough, the material used for the container makes a difference. Red-top glass tubes, for example, contain no chemicals. Red-top plastic tubes contain a clot-activator only. If you can remember what color the tube-top was, let your attorney know. However, your attorney should be able to examine the blood kit.

C. Site cleansing

The phlebotomist disinfects the draw site with povidone iodine unless the person is allergic to iodine. If so, then another non-alcoholic cleansing agent should be used (benzylkoniun chloride is a common substitute). Wiping must be done in concentric circles moving outward from the intended puncture site, otherwise the bacteria is just being pushed around, not removed. "Dry-swabbing" has been reported throughout the country. Dry-swabbing is a technique in which the phlebotomist uses a dry, sterile cloth to rub the area prior to the blood draw. This is not an accepted technique among phlebotomists and medical personnel. It can cause infection and contaminate the blood sample. It has developed, however, to thwart defense arguments that the disinfecting agent may contain alcohol. Your attorney definitely needs to know if you were the victim of dry-swabbing.

If the phlebotomist does not wipe the area properly, bacteria (Candida Albicans) can be sucked into the blood tube. Candida is everywhere. It is a yeast. When yeast and sugars (as in blood) mix, there could be fermentation, creating ethyl alcohol. This is indistinguishable from the ethyl alcohol allegedly consumed. The blood tube, however, could be tested for presence of Candida.

D. The blood draw

The phlebotomist will thread the safety needle supplied with the kit onto the hub until it is firmly seated. The first tube is then placed into the hub, but not far enough to puncture the seal. The vein is then punctured, and the tube is pushed further into the hub, breaking the seal and allowing blood to be sucked into the tube. Although it is uncommon, a phlebotomist may improperly seat the tube inside the hub and on the needle. This could result in an incompletely punctured stopper which will not allow any blood to flow, or a partially punctured stopper which will allow a small amount to flow and draw in outside air. The needle may also be bent, causing further problems.

The phlebotomist must also take care to insert the needle all the way into the vein, so as to prevent leakage of blood into the surrounding tissue, but not far enough to puncture both vein walls. The end of the needle is beveled for ease of insertion, but care must be taken to ensure that the bevel does not "seal" against the inner wall of the vein, causing obstructed blood flow.

The phlebotomist must keep the tube at a slight angle downward, so gravity will help prevent any backflow of the tube's contents into the subject's vein. This is a highly unlikely scenario because of blood pressure and vacuum, but backflow of chemicals from the tube into the subject could have disastrous results for the subject. The latex band should be removed as soon as blood begins to flow.

Once the first tube is filled, it should be removed and replaced with a second tube. When filled, the second tube should be removed from the hub and then the needle from the arm. The second tube can be contaminated when the phlebotomist withdraws the needle from the arm without withdrawing the second tube from the hub first. This will draw outside air, including Candida into the second tube only. Some blood kit instruction sheets actually show the incorrect way to draw blood, causing contamination in this manner. Most phlebotomists and police do not distinguish the first tube drawn from the second tube drawn.

E. Tube inversion

The tubes are supposed to be gently inverted at least eight times immediately after the draw to mix the preservative and anti-coagulant. Note: Many blood kit instructions direct the phlebotomist not to shake the vials. This is for personal safety, as blood may splatter from vigorous shaking. Integrity of the blood sample may also be affected by vigorous shaking which may cause the red blood cells to rip apart. If the cells are ripped apart, the whole blood sample becomes more like a plasma sample which can cause a higher reported BAC.

The chemicals have to mix with the blood in a proper proportion, otherwise they do not work properly. Too much blood or too little chemical and the blood could ferment, causing alcohol to form. Too little blood or too much chemical, and the chemicals could "salt out" the blood, causing a higher alcohol concentration under certain circumstances. Be sure to tell your attorney whether you remember the phlebotomist or the cop inverting the tubes.

F. Chain of custody and proper specimen handling

The preservative is supposed to prevent *endogenous formation* of alcohol, but lesser-strength solutions available will slow, but not stop, endogenous alcohol formation. Studies show that a 2% solution will stop the growth of Candida Albicans. Likewise, refrigeration only slows the decomposition, it does not stop it. Milk has preservatives added, yet it goes bad after a while even when refrigerated. Freezing will stop endogenous formation of alcohol, but Vacutainer® tubes used for law enforcement blood kits are glass and breakage becomes a problem. Generally, 4°C has been found to be a good compromise temperature for storage. Certainly, inquiries as to whether the blood remained in an unrefrigerated police car for some period of time should be made. In some jurisdictions, it is not uncommon to mail the blood sample to a crime lab. *Chain of custody* is always worth investigating.

The blood storage facility at the crime lab should be investigated. Access and inventory control can be decisive, yet simple, issues in a blood test case.

G. Laboratory Preparation of the Blood Sample

At the crime lab, the blood is taken out of the refrigerator and allowed to come to room temperature. Usually the tube is placed in a rocker that gently rocks the contents back and forth, ensuring a good mix. What exactly was the room temperature? Generally, we don't know. Often, the analysts let the samples sit for a couple of hours to get to room temperature. They say that this cannot harm the mixture, but would you leave milk out for two hours, even though it has preservatives in it? The second tube of blood should be repackaged and returned to the refrigerator in a timely manner. Due process issues may arise where the crime lab spoils the second sample.

Paperwork tracking the sample should be examined closely. Often, this will be reflected in the *Analyst's Bench Notes*. Some labs assign a bar code label to each blood kit and each tube as blood is transferred. Tracking the blood from the tube to the actual computer-generated BAC printout is very important.

Once the tube is at room temperature, the top is removed by either cutting it off or pulling it out of the tube. Care must be taken either way as cutting requires the use of a sharp instrument and pulling could cause splatter. It should always be done under an exhaust hood, and adequate protective measures should be taken to avoid contact with the blood.

Once the top is removed, the contents are poured into a container. A measured amount is removed from the container via a *pipette*. Ideally, the pipette should be electronic rather than manual to ensure greater accuracy and reliability. Maintenance and calibration records should be available for the pipette. Pipettes can be checked for accuracy by drawing a known amount of distilled water and depositing it onto a scale to check its weight.

The blood removed from the pipette is then transferred to a *headspace vial*. More sophisticated labs have pipettes that also draw a measured amount of *internal standard* and transfer the internal standard to the same headspace vial simultaneously with the blood. Two samples of blood should be prepared for testing, and the results should agree with each other to some adequate degree. Any somewhat competent lab should have no more than a 5% disagreement between samples.

The pipette must be rinsed clean between samples to avoid cross contamination from previous blood samples. Only de-ionized water should be used to rinse the pipette because the flame ionization detector (FID) at the end of the process counts ions that hit it, counting them as alcohol. One would not want to introduce ions that could interfere with the result.

The headspace vials are often placed into an autosampler, which is an automated rack that will move each vial into place for sampling. The use of an autosampler allows the analyst to set the machine to run samples without the need to be present to inject each sample. The autosampler also heats and shakes the vials to ensure proper mixing of the components. Check the time at which your client's sample was injected. It might be well after working hours and leads to a good area of cross-examination for your attorney.

3.6 Headspace Gas Chromatography

Chromatography is a separation science. It relies on chemical or mechanical means of separating substances into more discrete units. Headspace gas chromatography is an indirect method of measuring the amount of a volatile substance contained in a liquid by measuring an equilibrated amount of the volatile substance in the headspace above the liquid.

Blood is prepared in a headspace vial by mixing it with a known amount of an internal standard (often a type of alcohol) as described above. The vial is crimp-sealed. The quality of the crimp at the top of the vial is important because it will be one factor that governs how much gas pressure builds up in the vial above the mixture.

The mixture is heated to a specific temperature in order to release the volatile compounds. The actual temperature is not as critical as the constancy of the temperature. Colder temperatures result in longer times for the volatiles to move into the gaseous phase.

As the vial is heated, a gas rises above the mixture in the headspace vial like steam might rise above a pot of boiling water. The content of that gas is dependent upon *Henry's Law of Partial Pressures*. If the crimp is not perfect, it will change the pressure and the content of the gas. If the temperature varies, varying amounts of the volatiles will move into the gaseous phase as compared to other headspace vials.

Henry's Law—Assume a closed system and constant temperature. After a period of time, some of the molecules of the liquid will have moved into the gaseous phase in the headspace above the liquid. The number of molecules that have passed into the gaseous phase will be directly proportional to the number of molecules remaining in the liquid.

If we keep the temperature constant and the pressure constant, some of the alcohol molecules and the internal standard molecules will have passed from the liquid state into the headspace gaseous state. If we can measure the number of molecules in the headspace then we can, by conversion, quantify the amount of alcohol in the blood below it. Since the internal standard is mixed into the sample in a known amount and moves into the headspace at a known rate, the alcohol molecules are measured as a ratio in relation to the internal standard molecules released into the headspace.

If the temperature is not perfect, it will change the content of the gas. If the pressure is not constant, it will change the content of the gas.

In addition to the temperature and pressure, there is another factor that governs how much alcohol rises into the gas—that is called the *partition ratio*. Differing substances will have differing partition ratios, dependant upon many things, including the specific gravity of the substance.

Hematocrit, which is different but related to partition ratio, is also important. Hematocrit is a measure of the proportion of solid components to liquid components in the blood. Higher hematocrit means more solids. When pressurized, higher hematocrit levels push more hydrophilic molecules, such as alcohol, out of the liquid and into the gas. This can give a higher reported result if the internal standard passes into the gaseous phase at a slower rate than the alcohol.

The column is a tube about as thin as a human hair and approximately 30 meters in length. It is heated in an oven inside the machine and is usually in a coil shape. The temperature in most headspace gas chromatographs used for blood testing is 60°C.

An autosampler gently shakes and heats the headspace vials as it moves each one under a syringe. The syringe moves downward and punctures the crimped seal at the top of the headspace vial. It sucks a small amount of the headspace gas out and injects it into a transfer tube. Always check maintenance logs for syringe changes. Frequent changes may show problems with the process. Sometimes the syringes become bent because they miss the headspace vial. This is important if it happens during a blood run, and the run is continued without starting over. This means that the blood run was stopped and restarted without using new calibrators and controls.

At the same time that the headspace gas is being drawn out of the vial, an inert carrier gas (usually helium) is also introduced. The quality and content of the carrier gas should be documented as well as the intervals at which the filters for the carrier gas are inspected and changed. Ask for documentation regarding the purchase of the helium. Balloon grade helium is different from ultra-high purity scientific grade helium.

Both the carrier gas and the headspace sample move through the transfer tube and a Y-splitter. Half the mixture flows through one column, while the other half flows through a second column. As the gases move through the column, the rate of flow of some molecules is slowed by chemical attraction to the column. Thus, separation is achieved over the course of several minutes. Each volatile compound has its own unique retention time. Retention times vary from column to column. Two columns from the same manufacturer, made to the same specifications will have different retention times for identical compounds.

It is important to realize that the column is designed to capture and slow molecules. In fact, the column has to be replaced every now and then because it gets packed with crud and blood from the samples. More often, however, the column needs to have its ends "clipped" with a file. Most problems with the column occur at either end and it can be remedied by removing the first or last inch of the column. This changes retention times.

At the other end of the column from the injector is a flame, powered by hydrogen gas, supplied by the state. The purity of the gas generally is not tested. Many labs create their own hydrogen supply with a hydrogen generator. The term *generator* is misleading as it does not actually create hydrogen, but separates it from other gaseous components.

The blood samples emerge (or *elute*) from the end of the column, striking the flame at a specific time. If we know how long it takes alcohol to move through the column and emerge at the end, we know that all substances that take the same amount of time are alcohol. The flame vaporizes every volatile substance in its path. The burnt and ionized particles stick to an oppositely charged detector which counts them by measuring the electrical energy as each ion hits. The electrical signal strength is measured.

The GC then makes a mathematical calculation, and converts the electrical signal to a peak on a chromatogram (a computer-generated graph with peaks representing the electrical signal strength of volatile substances as they are ionized in the FID). There should be chromatograms for every sample introduced to the column. Eventually, the blood alcohol report is generated and printed.

The mathematical calculation is unknown to the analyst because it is proprietary information that belongs to the manufacturer of the machine. The area underneath the peak represents the signal strength. One can calculate the peak area using geometry and algebra to check the result. One can also cut the peaks out with scissors and weigh them on a scale to calculate the results (assuming constant paper thickness, a very accurate scale, and extreme precision in cutting out the peaks from the graph). The amount of alcohol that is being detected is so small that it cannot be seen with the human eye.

Each time the GC is run, it must "learn" what differing levels of alcohol look like. Generally, four calibrators are used to "teach" the machine to recognize 0.01%, 0.10%, 0.20% and 0.30% alcohol concentrations. Calibrators are used for this purpose and are commercially available or may be made in the lab. The important issue in calibration is to run the calibrators first and then to run "verifiers" at the end of the run. The verifiers should, of course, be at the same levels as the calibrators (0.01%, 0.10%, 0.20% and 0.30%) but must come from a different source. If they do not come from a different source, and a calibrator is incorrect, the verifier will not catch the mistake. It will simply confirm the earlier mistake as being accurate.

The calibration run will generate a *calibration curve report* which is a graphical representation of the ratio of internal standard peak size versus alcohol peak size. All subject samples can, and should, be plotted on the calibration curve report to check for accuracy.

Blanks must be run between samples at regular intervals to ensure no cross contamination from one sample to the next. *Controls*, which are blood samples of a known value, should also be run at regular intervals with the blanks to ensure that the GC is operating accurately. Controls are commercially available or may be made in the lab. Either way, documentation should be available for each control batch. A *standard mix*, made up of at least seven volatile compounds including ethanol, and internal standard must be run to ensure that the columns can separate different compounds.

3.7 Should I Have My Blood Re-tested or Have My Own Test Done?

A. Independent test versus referee sample

Before you can make any decision about secondary testing, you need to understand that there are two types of secondary testing. The terms *independent test* and *referee sample* (also known as a "*second sample*" or "*split*") are two very different things. Although an independent sample is commonly blood, it does not necessarily have to be a blood sample (it could be breath). The key to an independent sample is that it is entirely separate from the police collection and testing procedures. In the case of blood, it requires a separate needle stick and collection tubes.

A referee sample, second sample or "split," is one of the two tubes of blood drawn by law enforcement. It will generally be placed in safekeeping by the police for your own use.

B. Independent Testing

If you are arrested for DUI, and your evidential breath test result is over the limit, but you believe that you were under the limit, you should go to the nearest hospital and have your blood drawn and tested. Be aware that this will not be cheap and that there may be issues with chain-of-custody. Be sure to have your blood drawn as soon as possible after you are released from custody. Do not let the police know that you are going to have your own test done. This may lead to a situation where the police try to obtain custody of the blood or the test results. Obviously, if you are in police custody and request an independent test, they will know about it, but that does not necessarily mean that they will obtain the results. Do not make any statements to the medical personnel other than the reason for the test. In other words, tell them that you were arrested for DUI and want an independent test, but do not discuss the facts of the case with them. They could be subpoenaed as witnesses against you.

Always let your attorney know if you have had an independent test done or if the police prevented you from having one done.

C. Referee Sample

When blood is drawn by the police, they preserve one tube for testing by the defense. Sometimes the police will serve a Notice of Destruction of Evidence on you when the blood is taken. The Notice will state that you have a specified period of time within which to pick up your sample for testing, otherwise it will be destroyed.

Do not pick it up. This is a decision that should be made by you, in consultation with your attorney. There are many good reasons why an innocent person might not want to pick up the referee sample. The first reason is that the government's test results might be below the limit. If you pick up your blood tube and have it tested, it may be over the limit due to contamination or poor testing procedures. Sometimes the government's analyst will make a mistake and report a lower-than-true result. You don't want to mess that up.

Secondly, the referee sample does not have the added safeguards of an independent test because it relies upon the phlebotomist designated by the police, the integrity of the law enforcement blood kit and the handling of the tubes by law enforcement before it is picked up by the defendant's designee. If the police contaminated your blood tubes in a manner which would cause a higher result, it might cause a higher result for both blood tubes.

Thirdly, the government's analyst will often pick the best looking of the two tubes of blood for governmental testing. One tube might have been leaking, or is partially filled, or clotted, or rotting. The government's analyst will leave that tube for your uses. This information should be obtained by your attorney prior to making any decision about whether to test the second tube.

When picking up the second sample for defense testing, it is important that neither the defense attorney nor the defendant pick up the tube. The second sample should be retrieved by a third party designated by the defense. It should be delivered directly to the lab that will do the additional testing. Many messenger services provide this service at a reasonable fee. Private investigators may also perform this service. If the defense attorney or the accused picks up the sample, he or she becomes a witness regarding chain of custody. If the defendant picks it up, he or she also becomes a necessary witness for admissibility and leaves open the possibility of tampering.

Chapter 4

Driver License Issues

4.1 Chapter Overview

This chapter is the most general of all. This is because the laws pertaining to DUI and license issues vary the most from state to state. Moreover, if you are accused of DUI in a state where you do not hold a drivers license, your home state may act to punish you as well. The interface between the courts and licensing authorities is the most complex and confusing of all DUI issues. Even experienced attorneys sometimes have difficulty in deciphering what will happen to a drivers license under certain circumstances, but that should not cause you, the client, to doubt your attorney's abilities. What should cause you concern is when your attorney is not sure of the license consequences ***and*** does not bother to do the research to find the correct answer.

4.2 Implied Consent Laws

In many, but not all states, when a motorist is cited for one or more types of DUI, the motorist is subject to the requirements of implied consent laws and must submit to a chemical test or tests. The term "implied consent" simply means that you have impliedly given your consent to be tested by simply driving on the roadways and being cited for DUI. This is different from "express consent" where you have agreed, in writing, to be tested if you are cited for DUI. Most people, whether they know it or not, have expressly agreed to be tested when arrested for DUI by applying for a drivers license.

Commercially-licensed drivers are often subject to different and more unforgiving implied consent laws than are non-commercial license holders.

In any DUI investigation, there are only three possibilities with regard to chemical testing. The first possibility is that the police do not invoke any implied consent laws and do not do any chemical testing of their own. This may have serious consequences to a driver accused of DUI and who is actually under a presumptive Blood Alcohol Content (BAC) limit. The driver may be entitled to be told of the possibility of independent testing options. In some jurisdictions, the failure of the police to advise the driver of independent testing options when implied consent is not invoked, and there is no police test, may lead to a dismissal of charges. In other jurisdictions, it may have no effect.

The second possibility is that the police use some other method of gathering chemical test evidence. This may be pursuant to a search warrant, local statutes, or simple consent of the driver. In some jurisdictions, where the driver is incapable of giving consent (for example, being unconscious), the laws may allow the police to take blood or other bodily fluids. Sometimes where blood is being drawn for medical purposes, the police may request a portion of that blood from the agency that drew the blood. In other jurisdictions, if the driver refuses to be tested, a search warrant may be obtained to force a blood draw.

The third, and most common possibility, is that the police invoke implied consent laws and conduct a chemical test.

When the police do invoke implied consent laws and do their own chemical test, there are three possible scenarios:

1. The driver is under the per se limit, but may still be prosecuted for DUI.
2. The driver submits and is at or over the presumptive limit. In this case, most licensing authorities take action against the driver. The action may be a simple restriction of driving privileges or a complete suspension. Past driving history will have an effect in every state.
3. The driver refuses to submit. In some states, there is no penalty whatsoever for refusing to take a chemical test. In other states, it is a crime to refuse. In most states, it is not a crime, but it will be used as evidence of guilt and will carry a very serious license suspension or revocation consequence. In some states, the driver may also be subjected to a forced blood draw if the police obtain a search warrant after refusal to submit to a chemical test.

The driver may challenge an order of suspension through one of many types of proceedings which vary from a hearing to a summary review. In some states the burden is on the police at a license-suspension hearing to prove that the facts which led up to the issuance of the suspension order are true. Thus, if the police fail to appear at the license suspension hearing, the default will vacate an order of suspension. In other states, the opposite is true. It is the burden of the driver to show fault with the order of suspension. Thus, if the petitioner (driver) fails to appear, the default upholds the order of suspension.

A. The Implied Consent Form

After arrest and prior to taking a chemical test many states require the police to read an Implied Consent form to the arrestee. Obviously, if the motorist is dead or unconscious, or otherwise incapable of consenting, the admonitions need not be read. The Implied Consent form will generally recount the state's legal requirements and consequences for submitting to or refusing a test. It should also contain a short notice of the driver's rights with regard to chemical testing, and appeal.

B. Order of Suspension: Notice

There are two typical ways the Order of Suspension is served. One manner is in person, and the other is by mail. In the case of a refusal to submit to a chemical test, or when the motorist submits and is over the limit, the law enforcement officer may take away the motorist's license, serve the motorist with an Order of Suspension and issue a temporary drivers license.

In the case of a blood test result which is over the limit, and for some states for breath tests as well, the notice will have to be delivered to the driver in some manner. This may take the form of personal service or first-class mail. Be wary of states where the licensing authority simply mails the notice to the driver at the driver's last-known address. Sometimes the licensing authority is not required to keep track of returned notices that are undeliverable. Proof that it was mailed is considered prima facie evidence that the driver received it and it is up to the driver to prove otherwise. In every state, it is the driver's responsibility to keep the licensing authority apprised of a current address.

4.3 Recantation of Refusal

A driver may be able to recant his or her refusal to take a chemical test, but such recantation is subject to specific facts to determine if it is a defense.

4.4 Right to Attorney Prior to Taking Chemical Test

One does not have the absolute right to speak with an attorney in every state prior to deciding whether to submit to a chemical test.

4.5 Time Computations

It is always best to file a request for a license suspension hearing as soon as possible to avoid any hassles. However, there are times when it may be strategically advantageous to delay the filing, thus allowing you to drive as long as possible before any pending suspension. State laws govern time computations with regard to filing a request for a license suspension hearing.

Be aware, however, that the failure to hold a timely hearing often does not divest the licensing authority of jurisdiction, unless the petitioner can show actual prejudice. There is a double standard because the failure to file timely for a hearing usually precludes the hearing from taking place. In other words, sometimes if the licensing authority does not hold a timely hearing, there is nothing that you can really do about it. But if you do not make a timely request, the hearing will not be granted.

4.6 Reinstatement

Reinstatement after a suspension does not often happen automatically. Most jurisdictions require some sort of reapplication and a fee. In fact, when it comes to fees, you can be sure that your state licensing authority will require one. Some states require completion of a substance abuse course or counseling as well. Be sure to ask your attorney about reinstatement fees and requirements.

A. SR-22 Insurance

"SR-22" is a term used in the insurance industry to describe a high-risk insurance requirement and usually is not defined in any statute. Whether you will be required to obtain SR-22 insurance or any surety bond is a question for your attorney.

4.7 Minors

Minors 18 to 21 years old (i.e., not juveniles) may be affected by the DUI laws in the same manner as adults and more harshly. Although most (but not all) states will treat a minor the same as an adult, the driver license authority will often have stricter penalties.

4.8 Out-of-State Licensees

In the case of an out-of-state driver, the law enforcement officer has no legal authority to confiscate the out-of-state license. This is because the license remains the property of the home state of the driver, and while an individual state may have the authority to suspend nonresident driving privileges, the state has no authority to confiscate a license issued by another sovereign entity. However, most states have adopted an interstate driver license compact which requires the reporting of certain offenses as described below. The effect of this compact is that the licensee's home state will be aware of any restriction imposed by any other state, which will allow the home state both to suspend the driver's license pending resolution of the other state's infractions and implement their own punishment if they choose to do so.

4.9 Driver License Compact

Driver License Compact
Article I
Findings and Declaration of Policy

(a) The party states find that:

(1) The safety of their streets and highways is materially affected by the degree of compliance with state and local ordinances relating to the operation of motor vehicles.

(2) Violation of such a law or ordinance is evidence that the violator engages in conduct which is likely to endanger the safety of persons and property.

(3) The continuance in force of a license to drive is predicated upon compliance with laws and ordinances relating to the operation of motor vehicles, in whichever jurisdiction the vehicle is operated.

(b) It is the policy of each of the party states to:

(1) Promote compliance with the laws, ordinances and administrative rules and regulations relating to the operation of motor vehicles by their operators in each of the jurisdictions where such operators drive motor vehicles.

(2) Make the reciprocal recognition of licenses to drive and eligibility therefor more just and equitable by considering the overall compliance with motor vehicle laws, ordinances and administrative rules and regulations as a condition precedent to the continuance or issuance of any license by reason of which the licensee is authorized or permitted to operate a motor vehicle in any of the party states.

Article II
Definitions

As used in this compact:

(a) "State" means a state, territory or possession of the United States, the District of Columbia, or the Commonwealth of Puerto Rico.

(b) "Home state" means the state which has issued and has the power to suspend or revoke the use of the license or permit to operate a motor vehicle.

(c) "Conviction" means a conviction of any offense related to the use or operation of a motor vehicle which is prohibited by state law, municipal ordinance or administrative rule or regulation, or a forfeiture of bail, bond or other security deposited to secure appearance by a person charged with having committed any such offense, and which conviction or forfeiture is required to be reported to the licensing authority.

Article III
Reports of Conviction

The licensing authority of a party state shall report each conviction of a person from another party state occurring within its jurisdiction to the licensing authority of the home state of the licensee. Such report shall clearly identify the person convicted, describe the violation, specifying the section of the statute, code or ordinance violated, identify the court in which action was taken, indicate whether a plea of guilty or not guilty was entered, or the conviction was a result of the forfeiture of bail, bond or other security, and shall include any special findings made in connection therewith.

Article IV
Effect of Conviction

(a) The licensing authority in the home state, for the purposes of suspension, revocation or limitation of the license to operate a motor vehicle, shall give the same effect to the conduct reported, pursuant to article III of this compact, as it would if such conduct had occurred in the home state, in the case of convictions for:

(1) Manslaughter or negligent homicide resulting from the operation of a motor vehicle.

(2) Driving a motor vehicle while under the influence of intoxicating liquor or a narcotic drug or under the influence of any other drug to a degree which renders the driver incapable of safely driving a motor vehicle.

(3) Any felony in the commission of which a motor vehicle is used.

(4) Failure to stop and render aid in the event of a motor vehicle accident resulting in the death or personal injury of another.

(b) As to other convictions, reported pursuant to article III, the licensing authority in the home state shall give such effect to the conduct as is provided by the laws of the home state.

(c) If the laws of a party state do not provide for offenses or violations denominated or described in precisely the words employed in subdivision (a) of this article, such party state shall construe the denominations and descriptions appearing in subdivision (a) hereof as being applicable to and identifying those offenses or violations of a substantially similar nature and the laws of such party state shall contain such provisions as may be necessary to ensure that full force and effect is given to this article.

Article V
Applications for New Licenses

Upon application for a license to drive, the licensing authority in a party state shall ascertain whether the applicant has ever held, or is the holder of a license to drive issued by any other party state. The licensing authority in the state where application is made shall not issue a license to drive to the applicant if:

(1) The applicant has held such a license, but the same has been suspended by reason, in whole or in part, of a violation and if such suspension period has not terminated.

(2) The applicant has held such a license, but the same has been revoked by reason, in whole or in part, of a violation and if such revocation has not terminated, except that after the expiration of one year from the date the license was revoked, such person may make application for a new license if permitted by law. The licensing authority may refuse to issue a license to any such applicant if, after investigation, the licensing authority determines that it will not be safe to grant to such person the privilege of driving a motor vehicle on the public highways.

(3) The applicant is the holder of a license to drive issued by another party state and currently in force unless the applicant surrenders such license.

Article VI
Applicability of Other Laws

Except as expressly required by provisions of this compact, nothing contained herein shall be construed to affect the right of any party state to apply any of its other laws relating to licenses to drive to any person or circumstance nor to invalidate or prevent any driver license agreement or other cooperative arrangement between a party state and a non-party state.

Article VII
Compact Administrator and Interchange of Information

(a) The head of the licensing authority of each party state shall be the administrator of this compact for his state. The administrators, acting jointly, shall have the power to formulate all necessary and proper procedures for the exchange of information under this compact.

(b) The administrator of each party state shall furnish to the administrator of each other party state any information or documents reasonably necessary to facilitate the administration of this compact.

Article VIII
Entry Into Force and Withdrawal

(a) This compact shall enter into force and become effective as to any state when it has enacted the same into law.

(b) Any party state may withdraw from this compact by enacting a statute repealing the same, but no such withdrawal shall take effect until six months after the executive head of the withdrawing state has given notice of the withdrawal to the executive heads of all other party states. No withdrawal shall affect the validity or applicability by the licensing authorities of states remaining party to the compact of any report of conviction occurring prior to the withdrawal.

Article IX
Construction and Severability

This compact shall be liberally construed so as to effectuate the purposes thereof. The provisions of this compact shall be severable and if any phrase, clause, sentence or provision of this compact is declared to be contrary to the constitution of any party state or of the United States or the applicability thereof to any government, agency, person or circumstance is held invalid, the validity of the remainder of this compact and the applicability thereof to any government, agency, person or circumstance shall not be affected thereby. If this compact shall be held contrary to the constitution of any state party thereto, the compact shall remain in full force and effect as to the remaining states and in full force and effect as to the state affected as to all severable matters.

Chapter 5

Driving Under the Influence of Drugs

5.1 Chapter Overview

Not every state has laws which cover driving under the influence of drugs. Drugged driving is an afterthought of traditional alcohol-related DUI. Drugged driving can be broken down into the following three categories.

5.2 Driving Under the Influence of Drugs While Impaired

Whether a drug is legal or not is generally not a bar to prosecution if the drug impairs your ability to drive a vehicle. Certainly it would be illegal to drive under the influence of marijuana if it affects your ability to drive, but it is also illegal to drive under the influence of a legally prescribed drug, such as codeine, if it impairs you. It is generally not illegal to drive with a prescribed drug, or legal over-the-counter drug in your system if you are unimpaired.

Clearly, this makes sense. If what you ingest makes you a danger to yourself or others while behind the wheel, then your State Legislature has an interest in banning such behavior.

Many people who are stopped and questioned about what they have ingested will rattle off numerous prescription drugs, thinking that because they are prescribed to them, they are immune to prosecution. Not so. If you are stopped by a police officer and questioned about any medications or drugs that you may have ingested, your first line of defense is to remain silent. Moreover, many drugs have interactions with alcohol and other drugs. Most carry warning labels on the side of the bottle as required by law. However, some do not. Side effects of drugs can vary from person to person. You should not drive or operate machinery until you know how a particular drug affects you.

5.3 Driving with an Illegal Drug in Your System

This category can be divided into two sections. The first is driving with an illegal drug that impairs your ability to drive and the second is simply driving with the illegal drug in your system.

Just like it is illegal to drive with a prescribed drug in your system that impairs you, it is illegal to drive with an illegal drug in your system that impairs you. The reasoning is the same: If what you ingest makes you a danger to yourself or others while behind the wheel, your State Legislature has an interest in banning such behavior.

Some states have made it illegal to drive with any illegal drug in your system, irrespective of the effect on the driver. The legislative logic is that if it is illegal to possess or use prohibited drugs, then it should be illegal to drive with those prohibited substances in your system. Clearly, the rational basis test used by courts across the country applies: Is there a rational relationship between the criminal act and the danger which it attempts to prevent? Logically, it would seem that there is no rational relationship if one is unimpaired, however most courts fail to see the logic.

5.4 Driving with a Metabolite in Your System

The first thing that most people ask is: What's a metabolite?

A metabolite is the breakdown product of anything that you ingest. Your body metabolizes food and drink into various proteins, sugars and carbohydrates that fuel your cells. Drugs are no different. However, some things that you ingest will not metabolize. If you have dinner at a fancy restaurant and are served a very expensive dessert that has 24-karat gold leaf on top, your body will not metabolize the gold and it will pass right through you in the usual course of human events. This is because gold is an element and cannot be broken down into any smaller part by your body. Likewise, if you were to eat a rock, it is unlikely that your body would contain sufficient enzymes to be able to metabolize the rock.

Prescribed drugs may be metabolized into specific chemical compounds to help cure an illness. Illegal drugs are also metabolized. For example, Delta-9 Tetrahydrocannabinol (THC) is the active compound in marijuana. THC is what gets you high. But the metabolite, 11-Nor-Delta-9 Tetrahydrocannabinol will not make anyone high. Yet in some states, it is illegal to drive with either the active drug or its metabolite in your system.

5.5 The Drug Recognition Evaluation (DRE)

A. Drug Evaluation Classification Program (DECP)

Just as the police have alcohol-specific DUI investigatory techniques, they also have a drugged-driving specific protocol at their disposal. Not all departments have taken advantage of the program, however. Many reasons exist for this. Some departments have no funding for DRE/DECP. Others would like it, but it seems like too much work. Still other jurisdictions have no need for it because their legislatures have not made it a crime to drive while under the influence of drugs.

Aspirin is a drug. Penicillin is a drug. Heroin is a drug. Only one of the three preceding examples will impair your ability to drive a car. While society has a very broad definition of the term "drug," the law enforcement community has a much more narrow definition:

> A drug is any substance, which, when taken into the human body, can impair the ability of the person to operate a vehicle safely.
>
> —Drug Evaluation and Classification Training, "The Drug Recognition Expert School," Student Manual, NHTSA, August 1999.

This is the definition that law enforcement works from and, for their purpose, it is a good working definition. Clearly, the focus is on the effect, not on the chemical composition of the substance. Alcohol is certainly included in the definition, but so are other substances not included in general society's definition. For example, one typically does not think of spray paint as a drug, but some people will spray it into a pail or a bag, then breathe the concentrated vapors to get high. This act is called "huffing."

Despite the prevalence of drug use in our society, drugged driving has very little comparative literature and studies as does alcohol-related driving behavior. Drugged driving also has far less statutory and case law throughout the nation. In many instances, it appears that drugged driving statutes were an afterthought by the legislatures throughout the nation. So too, it seems that detection and prevention measures were afterthoughts. One only has to look at the 12-Step Drug Recognition Evaluation to see that the first step is to determine the suspect's Blood Alcohol Concentration (BAC) via a breath testing device. If the person's BAC is consistent with the level of impairment noted by the officer, then a Drug Recognition Evaluation will not ensue.

Additionally, because of the wide array of drugs available, it takes special and costly training to diagnose and identify impairment. On a practical level, not many departments have the resources to train many officers as "DREs" (Drug Recognition Experts). Moreover, because many people who use drugs other than alcohol often combine their use with alcohol, officers might recognize the impairment resulting from drugs other than the alcohol. An officer might easily declare a person with a low BAC, but high level of impairment, as a "lightweight" and not think to check further for drug-induced impairment.

B. The Three-Step DRE Process

The "Three-Step DRE Process" as explained by NHTSA in every DRE manual published to date, is a simple one which encompasses the 12-Step DRE Protocol explained in full detail later in this chapter.

The Three-Step DRE Process:

1. Verify that the suspect is impaired and verify that the suspect's BAC is inconsistent with the degree of impairment evident.
2. Determine whether the impairment is drug or medical related.
3. Use proven diagnostic procedures to determine the category of drugs that is the likely source of impairment.

Note that the first obligation is to determine BAC and make a very subjective determination as to whether the level of impairment matches the suspect's BAC. The proper interpretation of the Standardized Field Sobriety Tests (SFSTs) correlates performance to a percentage chance that the subject is at or above a particular BAC. So if an officer administers the SFSTs properly and sees, for example, four out of six cues on the Horizontal Gaze Nystagmus Test (HGN), two on the Walk-and-Turn and two on the One-Leg-Stand, that officer should conclude that the person's BAC is at or above .080, based on his training. If the person's BAC is only .020, that should be an indication to the officer that there is another cause for the impairment. Yet because of problems with the validity of the SFST studies, the individual predilections of the officers and training issues, the objectivity of the DRE process becomes subverted in many instances.

The second obligation is for the officer to "play doctor" and make medical determinations. Even some of the most brilliant doctors in the world may have problems separating medically related impairment issues from drug-induced impairment when given only the tools used by law enforcement, by the side of the road and under less than ideal examination conditions. Frankly, it is unreasonable to put such a burden on law enforcement personnel with minimal training and, in many instances, little formal education.

The third step is for the officer to "use proven diagnostic procedures to determine the category of drugs that is the likely source of impairment." NHTSA refers to "proven diagnostic procedures" as if they have actually been proven. They have not. Like the SFST studies, the DRE studies generally have not been peer reviewed as a whole. Certainly individual parts of the 12-Step DRE Protocol have proven scientific validity, but there is very little evidence, if any, to suggest that the entire protocol has validity. Even the DRE workshop called for by the *NHTSA Training Manual* is highly flawed. One glaring problem is that the training (Section XII of the manuals) calls for an alcohol workshop, not a drug workshop. In other words, volunteers are dosed with varying amounts of alcohol and not other drugs before they are examined. This means that the police only get to see what a central nervous system depressant (alcohol) does to a person. From a practical standpoint, one can understand the reasons behind not dosing volunteers with PCP for a law enforcement workshop, yet that still does not alleviate the problem resulting from the workshop—that the police leave the workshop with no real examples of impairment via drugs other than alcohol.

C. The 12-Step DRE Protocol

The following 12-Step DRE Protocol is taken from *Drug Evaluation and Classification Training, The Drug Recognition Expert School*, 2002 Student Edition.

Drug Influence Report Checklist

_____ 1. Breath Alcohol test
_____ 2. Interview of Arresting Officer
(Note: Gloves must be worn from this point on.)
_____ 3. Preliminary Examination and First Pulse
_____ 4. Eye examinations
_____ 5. Divided Attention Tests:
________ Romberg Balance
________ Walk-and-Turn
________ One-Leg-Stand
________ Finger-to-Nose
_____ 6. Vital Signs and Second Pulse
_____ 7. Dark Room Examinations and Ingestion Examination
_____ 8. Check for Muscle Tone
_____ 9. Check for Injection Sites and Third Pulse
_____ 10. Interrogation, Statements, and Other Observations
_____ 11. Opinion of Evaluator
_____ 12. Toxicological Evaluation

1. Breath Alcohol test—to determine the suspect's blood alcohol concentration (BAC).

By obtaining an accurate and immediate measurement of BAC, the drug recognition expert can determine whether alcohol may be contributing to the suspect's observable impairment, and whether the concentration of alcohol is sufficient to be the sole cause of that impairment.

It is always possible that a person suspected of being under the influence of drugs other than alcohol may actually have consumed only alcohol. However, it is also very common to find that a suspect has consumed alcohol and other drugs.

2. Interview of arresting officer—to take advantage of the things that he or she may have seen or heard during earlier contact with the suspect.

Most arresting officers are not as knowledgeable about drugs as are drug recognition experts. The arresting officers may have uncovered some drug paraphernalia, or overheard the suspect using drug-related "street" terms, without recognizing their significance. A few minutes spent in a careful discussion with the arresting officer can alert the drug recognition expert to the most promising areas of investigation to be explored with the suspect.

3. The preliminary examination, which is a structured series of questions, specific observations and simple tests that provide the first opportunity to examine the suspect closely and directly. **Note: to avoid infection, the drug recognition expert must wear gloves from this portion of the examination on.**

One major purpose of the preliminary examination is to determine if the suspect may be suffering from an injury or some other condition not necessarily related to drugs. Another major purpose is to begin systematically assessing the suspect's appearance, behavior, etc. for signs of possible drug influence.

4. The examination of the eyes, which include Horizontal Gaze Nystagmus, Vertical Gaze Nystagmus, and a check for Lack of Convergence.

Nystagmus will be caused with certain categories of drugs. Nystagmus, an involuntary jerking that may occur as the eyes gaze to the side or as they are elevated. The presence of nystagmus, and the points at which it becomes observable, can shed light on the possible presence of those categories and the extent to which they may be affecting the suspect.

The inability of the eyes to converge toward the bridge of the nose also gives evidence of the possible presence of certain categories of drugs.

5. Divided attention psychophysical tests, which include the Romberg Balance; the Walk-and-Turn; One-Leg-Stand; and, the Finger-to-Nose.

The suspect's performance of these tests produces articulable evidence of their psychophysical impairment. The specific errors of omission or commission may point towards the categories of drugs that are behind that impairment.

6. Vital signs examinations, which include systematic checks of the suspect's blood pressure; pulse rate; and, temperature.

Certain categories of drugs may elevate blood pressure, pulse rate and raise the body temperature. Other drugs would have precisely the opposite effects. Vital signs as well as physical observations thus provide valuable evidence of the presence and influence of a variety of drug categories.

7. Dark room examinations, which include systematic checks of the size of the pupils of the suspect's eyes; the reaction of the pupils to light; and, evidence of ingestion of drugs by nose or mouth.

Certain categories of drugs affect the eyes, and especially the pupils, in predictable ways. By examining the eyes under carefully controlled lighting conditions, important evidence of those drug categories may be obtained.

8. Examination for muscle tone. Certain categories of drugs will cause the muscles to become rigid. Some other categories may cause the muscles to become flaccid.

Begin with the left arm, firmly grasp the upper arm and slowly moving down to determine whether the muscle tome is flaccid, normal or rigid.

9. Examination for injection sites, e.g., via hypodermic needles.

Users of certain categories of drugs routinely or occasionally ingest their drugs via injection. Evidence of Needles use (scars, "tracks", etc.) may be found on veins along the neck, arms, legs, etc.

10. Suspect's statements and other observations. Based on the nine previous components of the drug examination, the drug recognition expert should have formed at least an articulable suspicion as to the category or categories of drugs that may be present. The expert then can proceed, *in full conformance with the suspect's Constitutional rights*, to attempt to interview the suspect concerning the drug or drugs involved.

11. Opinions of the evaluator. Based on all of the evidence and observations obtained during the previous ten steps, the drug recognition expert should be able to reach an informed opinion concerning:

Whether the suspect is under the influence of a drug or drugs; and if so, the category or combination of categories of drugs that is the probable cause of the suspect's impairment.

These conclusions should be documented, along with a narrative capsule summary of the observed facts that led to the conclusions.

12. The toxicological examination, which is a chemical test or tests that can provide scientific, admissible evidence to substantiate the drug recognition expert's conclusions.

D. Deconstruction and Analysis of the 12-Step DRE Protocol

Step 1: Breath Alcohol test

Note that there is neither a standard as to what type of breath alcohol test must be used for Step 1 nor any type of guideline as to what an acceptable BAC would be to determine whether the DRE will continue with the DRE investigation or treat the case as an alcohol-related DUI.

Under the protocol, it is quite possible that the officer might use an unapproved, uncalibrated device for determination of BAC. Moreover, since there is no guide as to what particular BAC would trigger the full 12-Step Protocol, it is left to the individual predilection of the DRE. Suppose the DRE obtains a BAC of .090; this would surely be enough to prosecute a driver for DUI. Yet, the DRE might feel that he needs some overtime hours on his next paycheck, so he launches into a full-blown DRE investigation. Yet another officer with the same facts might not do the DRE. This leads to unequal enforcement of the laws and a possible due process violation.

Step 2: Interview of the arresting officer

Many times the DRE is not the one who makes the initial stop or arrest of the driver. The stop officer is supposed to be interviewed by the DRE. Clearly, the most helpful information would be if the stop officer observed the smell of burning marijuana at the stop or had some other plain indicia of ingestion, especially statements by the driver. Be wary of the fact that the stop officer's statements to the DRE might guide the DRE to a particular conclusion. It is very helpful to note the actual signs of impairment gathered by the DRE and compare them with the end result. Many times you will find that the DRE's opinion matches the type of drug that the driver admitted to ingesting but does not match the conclusion demanded by the results of the protocol.

Another area to watch is probable cause for the arrest. If the driver is already under arrest at the time of the arrival of the DRE, examine the probable cause for that arrest. Sometimes you will find that the person has been placed under arrest for DUI-Drugs before the 12-Step Protocol has begun. This is problematic for the prosecution, to say the least. Examination of the arresting officer should be complete and demanding. If the arresting officer is not a DRE and determined that the driver had a .000 BAC but should be placed under arrest for DUI nonetheless, what was the probable cause?

Step 3: Preliminary examination

The protocol states that the preliminary examination uses "a structured series of questions, specific observations and simple tests" without further definition. This leaves the contents of the section up to the discretion of each officer, agency and jurisdiction. Since this protocol is supposed to be standardized and obtains its alleged validity from that standardization, Step 3 leaves the defense attorney ample opportunity to attack admissibility.

Step 4: Examination of the eyes

The results of these tests should be no more admissible under the DRE Protocol than they would be under a traditional alcohol-related DUI investigation. Even if HGN is admissible under certain circumstances in an alcohol-related DUI, the physiological mechanism for causation by drugs is entirely different. Horizontal Gaze Nystagmus, Vertical Gaze Nystagmus, and Lack of Convergence need appropriate expert medical testimony to pass the admissibility test.

Step 5: Divided attention psychophysical tests

Note that the Romberg Balance and the Finger-to-Nose tests are not NHTSA validated tests. The Walk-and-Turn and One-Leg-Stand have only been validated by NHTSA for alcohol-related purposes (specifically related to a particular BAC). Yet the DRE uses them to diagnose impairment—not any specific level of drug. And in all cases, none of the tests has been published in peer reviewed articles as having the validity claimed by NHTSA.

Step 6: Vital signs examinations

While checks of the suspect's blood pressure, pulse rate and temperature are not new or novel, having someone evaluate these vital signs and interpret them as part of a DRE is new and novel. Alcohol and other drugs can certainly cause a neurological impairment as can other organic causes such as a brain tumor or chemical imbalance within the body. Police officers are no more qualified to diagnose alcohol and drug impairment than they are to diagnose a brain tumor.

Step 7: Dark room examinations

DREs are supposed to use a pupillometer to compare the suspect's pupil size with a standard. A pupillometer is nothing more than a card with differing sizes of dots arranged in an ascending order from smallest to largest. Generally, a pupillometer will start at 1 mm and move in half-millimeter increments to about 9 mm, although there is no standard for a pupillometer. Note that if a pupillometer is a photocopy of another pupillometer, the size of the dots may have varied through the photocopy process. A reliable pupillometer will be an engraved card that has had each of the dots verified by measurement.

A dark room examination can be quite dangerous for an officer. He will be in an enclosed, dark space, and in very close proximity to a suspect who may be high on drugs with unpredictable effects. Violence might certainly occur. This is why the NHTSA manual always requires a back-up officer in the room while the DRE performs the evaluation.

The effect on the suspect might also be affected by the close quarters and intensive examination. Someone who is anxious or hypertensive might be even more so because of this portion of the examination. It is realistic to expect an already nervous person to experience a heart rate increase and produce more perspiration. These are signs easily mistaken for the effects of drugs.

Step 8: Examination for muscle tone

Note that there is no standard for determination as to whether the muscle tone is flaccid, normal or rigid.

Step 9: Examination for injection sites

Certainly evidence of injection sites can provide valuable information for the DRE, but the DRE must be able to distinguish between recent and old sites, along with normal abrasions to the skin.

Step 10: Suspect's statements and other observations

Compare carefully the results of this step (as well as Step 2) with the end result. Many times the 12-Step Protocol will lead to the conclusion that the suspect is under the influence of a category of drugs that are entirely inconsistent with the opinion of the evaluator, yet consistent with what the suspect admitted to ingesting.

Step 11: Opinions of the evaluator

Watch for broad conclusions that ignore the signs and symptoms recorded by the officer. Also note that sometimes an individual step is ignored in the process.

Step 12: Toxicological examination

Note that the toxicological examination is the culmination of the 12-Step Protocol and is used to confirm the DRE's opinions. It is helpful to gather the results of toxicological exams from other DRE examinations done by the same officer and calculate a percentage of competence for the officer.

5.6 Nationwide DRE Laws

Some states have no laws against driving while under the influence of drugs. Yet even in states where such laws exist, one cannot simply assume that the 12-Step DRE Protocol is admissible in every jurisdiction. Even in jurisdictions where it has been admitted, there is still room to challenge further admissibility and conclusions drawn from the DRE testimony. The following is a compilation of precedent setting law from around the nation regarding admissibility of DRE testimony, in chronological order. Many states have never addressed the issue on any precedent setting level. Your attorney may want to review these cases:

> *People v. Quinn*, 158 Misc.2d 1015 (1993) New York, 1993. The defense submitted the matter to a judge on stipulated facts rather than face a jury in order to challenge the DRE Protocol on appeal. The case was reversed, however, because there was no waiver of a jury before submission on stipulated facts. Thus, the court did not consider the questions regarding the scientific reliability of a Drug Influence Evaluation. Yet the court felt obliged to write: "However, we would note that in light of the overwhelming evidence of guilt, any error in admitting such testimony would clearly be harmless."
>
> *State v. Klawitter*, 518 N.W.2d 577 (1994) Minnesota, 1994. Visual exam to determine nystagmus and convergence is scientific in nature but satisfies the *Frye* requirement. The remainder of the 12-Step DRE Protocol is not scientifically new and, therefore, is not subject to *Frye*. The court specifically found that the 12-Step Protocol is "essentially the same components that are used by police officers in evaluations for alcohol impairment or are routine examinations that can be competently performed by the police officer."
>
> One thing to keep in mind—the officer involved in this case was qualified to take medical vital signs and do an examination because he was a certified EMT.
>
> The dissent is great. It finds that while the individual 12 steps are not new or novel, basing an opinion upon them is new and novel. The dissent reminds the rest of the court that the prosecution relies on the totality of the circumstances—not on 12 individual steps, isolated from each other.
>
> *U.S. v. Everett*, 972 F.Supp. 1313 (1997) Nevada, 1997. DRE testimony is not scientific in nature; it is based upon observations, training and experience and, therefore, is governed by Rule 702, not *Daubert*. The federal court wrote: "the otherwise qualified DRE cannot testify as to scientific knowledge, but can testify as to "specialized knowledge which will assist the trier of fact to understand the evidence."
>
> *Williams v. State*, 710 So.2d 24 (1998) Florida, 1998. The court concluded that the 12-Step DRE Protocol is not subject to *Frye* because

tests are within the common experience and understanding of the average person and are not scientific within the meaning of *Frye*. The court wrote: "Contrary to the defendant's assertion, The DRE's opinion is not derived from the symptomology matrix and does not constitute a medical diagnosis."

Horizontal Gaze Nystagmus (HGN), Vertical Gaze Nystagmus (VGN) and Lack Of Convergence (LOC) are scientific within the meaning of *Frye*, but *Frye* does not apply because the tests are not new or novel. However, they do not immunize particular areas or principles based on longevity, but go on to say that longevity is helpful to exclude certain evidence from *Frye* analysis which would be wasteful of judicial resources. The court cites to the Minnesota case, *Klawitter*.

State v. Baity, 140 Wash.2d 1, 991 P.2d 1151 (2000) Washington, 2000. DRE Protocol meets *Frye*'s requirements, although many of the DRE steps are not scientific. HGN is scientific but is generally accepted and satisfies *Frye* requirements. With regard to DRE testimony, the court wrote: "This Court finds that the DRE can testify to the probabilities, based upon his or her observations and clinical findings, but cannot testify by way of scientific opinion, that the conclusion is an established fact by any reasonable scientific standard."

The court cautioned that their opinion is confined to situations where all 12 steps of the DRE protocol have been used.

State v. Sampson, 167 Or.App. 489, 6 P.3d 543 (2000) Oregon, 2000. DRE protocol and testimony are scientific evidence and admissible because they have achieved a significant degree of acceptance within the relevant scientific community to be sufficiently established. Scientific parts of the DRE include the following: BAC, VGN, LOC, vital signs, toxicological analysis. Other parts of the DRE are not scientific, yet admissible.

Evidence of the DRE examination is not more highly prejudicial than probative of any fact.

State v. Aman, 194 Or.App. 463, 95 P.3d 244 (2004) Oregon, 2004. Incomplete 12-Step DREs are not admissible as scientific evidence. In this case the urine sample was not taken because the defendant could not produce one. Reversed and remanded. Note that the state admitted that toxicology results do not directly relate to a suspect's impairment but furnish only circumstantial evidence to corroborate a DRE officer's opinion.

Chapter 6

The Court Process

6.1 Chapter Overview

The courtroom drama that you will be exposed to is nothing like the courtroom drama that you might see on television. Surprise witnesses, investigations that take place during the trial and judges that are always right are simply unrealistic. Moreover, most apprehension comes from the unknown process that will take place. This chapter examines the court process and what you can expect. It should serve as a guide for you to ask intelligent questions of your attorney. As always, rely on your attorney's specific advice.

6.2 How Should I Act?

Always show respect for the judge, the jury and the court staff. Keep in mind that you are "on display" from the moment that you walk out of the front door of your house to go to court. You may encounter a potential juror, court staff or the judge in the parking lot of the courthouse. Always be courteous. Always be on time. Defense attorneys across the country cringed when Michael Jackson appeared for court late for the second time, and wearing pajamas. One can only speculate as to why the judge did not throw him in jail. Keep in mind, however, that you are not Michael Jackson.

During trial or hearings, it is best not to visibly react to what is going on in the courtroom. Sometimes something funny will happen in the courtroom, even during the most serious of proceedings. People, including the judge and jury may laugh or chuckle. You may do so as well, but don't be the only one. However, one thing that should never be done by the accused is to be disrespectful of a witness. It is common knowledge that many cops lie on the stand. In fact, the term "testilying" was coined by the police. Even if the arresting officer is making false statement after false statement, you should not visibly react. You should certainly make a note of it and pass it to your attorney, or quietly whisper something in his ear about it, but don't make a scene or roll your eyes, or sigh in disgust.

While at the counsel table, sit up straight. Don't slouch. Don't chew your fingernails, pick your nose or play with your hair. Your attorney should provide you with a notepad and pen. Take notes. Even if you don't want to take notes, at least pretend that you are taking notes. Jurors don't like to see someone who seems disinterested in his or her trial.

Always rise upon entrance of the judge into the courtroom and remain standing until you are told to be seated. Rise when the judge leaves the courtroom and remain standing until the judge has left.

You will likely be under direct and specific orders from the judge not to speak to jurors during your trial. It is best that you avoid them at all times. You might find yourself waiting for the elevator with a juror. I always advise my clients to wait for another elevator. Sometimes you might find yourself in the same restaurant as one or more jurors during the lunch break. Ask for a table away from them. If that is impossible, consider going to another restaurant. The idea is to not even show the appearance of impropriety.

Never contact the judge or the prosecutor yourself. In many cases it might be illegal to speak to the judge without opposing counsel being present. In *every* case it is a dumb idea to speak to the judge without your counsel being present. The prosecutor is your enemy. The prosecutor will use everything at his or her disposal to try to convict you. You cannot talk your way out of the DUI. If that was a possibility, your attorney would have likely done so.

6.3 How Should I Dress?

Conservatively. Unless your attorney advises you otherwise, in court men and women should wear a dark business suit. Dress as if you are applying for a job at IBM or some other large corporation. Men should trim their facial hair neatly or shave it off. Jurors most often have a negative bias against men with facial hair. Earrings and jewelry other than a wedding ring should be removed. Leave the nose-ring at home and use makeup to cover the hole as best as possible. Tattoos should be covered as best as possible. Wear a tan, white or light blue dress shirt. Your tie should be dark and not have any mottos, insignia or crests on it.

Women should wear makeup conservatively. Blouses should not be low-cut and they should be buttoned up properly (minimize the cleavage). Leave the expensive jewelry at home. Skirts are preferable to pants, but your skirt should not be above the knee. Body-color or sheer stockings should be worn. Hair can be worn up or down, but should not look out of place. Cover any tattoos as best as possible. I know that this is sexist advice, but your jury trial is neither the time nor the place to challenge sexist stereotypes. You can do that once you are released by the court.

Please remember that this advice is probably the most variable of any in this book. Your attorney will know the local customs better than I do. The important thing to do is to ask your attorney about how you should dress for court.

6.4 Initial Appearance

An initial appearance is also known as an arraignment. It is at this time that the judge will ask you to enter a plea of Guilty or Not Guilty. There is rarely any good reason to plead guilty at an arraignment. You are not O.J. Simpson. Do not plead "100% Not Guilty" or make any other cute remark. You can answer the judge's questions with simple yes-or-no answers. The judge at your arraignment may be, but is not necessarily going to be your trial judge. Be aware that in some jurisdictions you have the right to have a different judge assigned to your case for no particular reason other than that you have requested the change in a timely manner. Be aware that local time limits will apply in such a situation.

Bond may be set at this time. The court will consider things such as whether you are likely to flee the jurisdiction, the seriousness of the offense, and whether there are any victims involved. Some jurisdictions have rules regarding specific no-bail offenses such as child-rape. DUI cases, however, generally have no specific rules.

6.5 Pretrial Motions

Pretrial motions can be broken down into three main categories: Procedural, Substantive, and Motions in Limine. Procedural motions must be filed in every case and are usually discovery related. Substantive motions are filed in an effort to suppress evidence and dismiss charges. Motions in Limine are filed immediately prior to trial and are usually aimed at limiting evidence at trial or allowing exploration of certain issues during questioning. Be aware that "Motions in Limine" often are not defined and may not be available in some jurisdictions.

A. Procedural Motions

Procedural motions must be filed in every case. The Notice of Appearance does exactly what the name suggests—it give the court notice of your attorney's appearance and will usually contain a plea of Not Guilty and may request a trial by jury where applicable.

The Notice of Defenses lists not only who the defense expects to call at trial, but also a simple statement of what that witness is expected to testify about. It is important to tell your attorney about all witnesses and any evidence that you know of, whether you think it is relevant or not. If your attorney does not disclose it, he or she will likely not be able to use it at trial.

The Discovery should address everything that the defense attorney could possibly require at trial. There is nothing preventing an attorney from filing a timely supplemental Notice of Defenses or Request for Discovery as circumstances change. You should receive copies of your attorney's motions as well as those filed by the state. Read them over and ask questions of your attorney if you have them. Keep in mind that the prosecution must also file these same motions.

B. Substantive Motions

1. Challenge to Grand Jury

A Grand Jury is made up of citizens who are empaneled to hear prosecutors present cases and then to make decisions as to whether the person accused should have to stand trial. Most often Grand Juries are held in secret. There is no defense attorney or judge present. Grand Juries are used almost exclusively for felony charges and not misdemeanors. Because grand juries do not determine guilt or innocence, defendants in grand jury proceedings are not entitled to all the protections that are afforded defendants in jury trials. So when the prosecution oversteps its bounds and makes an improper presentation to the Grand Jury, a defense attorney may challenge the indictment on the grounds that the accused was denied a substantial procedural right.

Upon hearing a motion challenging the Grand Jury indictment, a judge may do one of three things (with regard to each charge). The judge may deny the challenge and allow the indictment to stand. The judge may remand the case to the Grand Jury for a new determination. Or, in very rare circumstances usually involving intentional misconduct on the part of the prosecutors, dismiss the case or specific charges.

2. Reasonable Suspicion

All traffic stops must be performed with reasonable suspicion that the driver has either violated the motor vehicle code or engaged in some type of criminal activity. Usually, if there is no violation of the motor vehicle code, the officer making the stop will claim that there was some sort of traffic movement which is legal, but gave him cause to believe that the driver was impaired or basis for some other reason for the stop. Generally, the police officer will refer to the NHTSA cues for detecting impaired drivers to justify the stop.

The defense, however, does not have to show that there were no such movements. The burden on the defense is simply to show that there was no warrant issued for the defendant's seizure on the date that he was detained and that he was, in fact, detained. At that point, the prosecutor must show that there was a valid exception to the Fourth Amendment's requirements for a warrantless seizure. A warrantless search is presumptively unreasonable under the Fourth Amendment to the United States Constitution and is subject only to a few specifically established, jealously and carefully drawn exceptions. *Jones v. United States*, 357 U.S. 493, 78 S.Ct. 1253.

An investigative stop will be deemed reasonable where the officer can demonstrate some basis from which the court can determine that the police were not arbitrary or harassing. *United States v. Walling*, 486 F.2d 229 (9th Cir. 1973), Cert. denied, 415 U.S. 923, 94 S.Ct. 1427, 39 L.Ed.2d 479 (1974). *United States v. Walling; Wilson v. Porter*, 361 F.2d 412, 415 (9th Cir. 1966); *United States v. Contreras-Diaz*, 575 F.2d 740 (9th Cir.), Cert. denied, 439 U.S. 855, 99 S.Ct. 167, 58 L.Ed.2d 161 (1978); Constitutional perimeters are spelled out in *Terry v. Ohio*, 392 U.S. 1, 88 S.Ct. 1868, 20 L.Ed.2d 889 (1968). There, the Supreme Court of the United States held that a police officer may effect a limited detention of an individual, not amounting to an arrest, if the officer's actions were reasonable under the circumstances.

"Terry requires a dual inquiry into the reasonableness of an investigatory stop. The reviewing court must determine: (1) whether the facts warranted the intrusion on the individual's Fourth Amendment rights, and (2) whether the scope of the intrusion was reasonably related "to the circumstances which justified the interference in the first place." *Carpenter v. Sigler*, 419 F.2d 169, 171 (8th Cir. 1969). *United States v. Stevie*, 578 F.2d 204, 207 (8th Cir. 1977).

An investigative detention is lawful if the officer is "able to point to specific and articulable facts which, taken together with rational inferences from those facts, reasonably warrant...[the officer's] intrusion" upon the person's Fourth Amendment rights." *Terry v. Ohio*, 392 U.S. 1, 21, 88 S.Ct. 1868, 1880, 20 L.Ed.2d 889, 906 (1968). If the totality of the circumstances provides a "particularized and objective basis" for the officers to suspect that the person is engaged in criminal activity, the stop is permissible. *United States v. Cortez*, 449 U.S. 411, 417, 101 S.Ct. 690, 695, 66 L.Ed.2d 621, 629 (1981)

Whether an officer's conduct was "reasonable" or "appropriate" depends on the facts and circumstances of the particular case, so that the decision in one case seldom furnishes a pat answer in another case. (Cites omitted.) A principle to be applied generally however is that in judging the reasonableness of the actions of the officer the circumstances before him are not to be dissected and viewed singly; rather they must be considered as a whole. So considered they are to be viewed through the eyes of a reasonable and cautious officer on the scene, guided by his experience and training. See *United States v. Davis*, 147 U.S.App.D.C. 400, 458 F.2d 819 (1972). *United States v. Hall*, 174 U.S.App.D.C. 13, 15, 525 F.2d 857, 859 (1976).

The Supreme Court of the United States in *Pennsylvania v. Mimms*, 434 U.S. 106, 108-09, 98 S.Ct. 330, 332, 54 L.Ed.2d 331, 335-36 (1977), set forth the test for Fourth Amendment violations in this fashion:

> "The touchstone of our analysis under the Fourth Amendment is always 'the reasonableness in all the circumstances of the particular governmental invasion of a citizen's personal security.' *Terry v. Ohio*, 392 U.S. 1, 19, 88 S.Ct. 1868, 20 L.Ed.2d 889 (1968). Reasonableness, of course, depends 'on a balance between the public interest, and the individual's right to personal security free from arbitrary interference by law officers.' *United States v. Brignoni-Ponce*, 422 U.S. 873, 878, 95 S.Ct. 2574, 45 L.Ed.2d 607 (1975)."

In the opinion of *Brown v. Texas*, --- U.S. ----, 99 S.Ct. 2637, 2640, 61 L.Ed.2d 357 (1979), the Supreme Court said that a central concern in balancing these competing considerations "has been to assure that an individual's reasonable expectation of privacy is not subject to arbitrary invasions solely at the unfettered discretion of officers." In applying the federal standard to the facts of this case, it becomes clear that the officer's actions were unreasonable.

Where a person has been seized unlawfully, an incidental search is also unlawful and fruits of the search are admissible and cannot be used against the person. *Wong Sun v. United States,* 371 U.S. 471, 83 S.Ct. 407, 9L.Ed.2d 441. Thus, any evidence obtained after the seizure must be suppressed.

3. Probable Cause

Once again, it is the State's burden to show that there is a valid exception to the search warrant requirement of the Fourth Amendment just as they had to do so for reasonable suspicion. Where a defendant shows that the search was warrantless, it is the State's burden to show a valid exception to the warrantless search requirement. The State carries the burden of proof as well as the burden of going forward with the evidence.

A warrantless search is presumptively unreasonable under the Fourth Amendment subject only to a few specifically established, jealously and carefully drawn exceptions. *Jones v. United States*, 357 U.S. 493, 78 S.Ct. 1253.

When the constitutional validity of an arrest is challenged, it is the function of a court to determine whether the facts available to the officers at the moment of the arrest would "warrant a man of reasonable caution in the belief" that an offense has been committed. *Carroll v. United States*, 267 U.S. 132, 162, 45 S.Ct. 280, 288, 69 L.Ed. 543.

Be mindful of the fact that even where the police have established reasonable suspicion, the driving behavior is still relevant to a determination of probable cause. Take, for example, the situation where a person is stopped for an equipment violation of having no license plate light, but was driving fine. Clearly, there is reasonable suspicion to stop, but having an inoperable license plate light has nothing to do with impairment. Driving well is an argument against impairment and such facts should be used by the defense. If the police have clearly insufficient evidence to believe that an offense had been committed, then the seizure was without probable cause.

> "An arrest without a warrant bypasses the safeguards provided by an objective predetermination of probable cause, and substitutes instead the far less reliable procedure on an after-the-event justification for the arrest or search, too likely to be subtly influenced by the familiar shortcomings of hindsight judgment."

Beck v. Ohio, 379 U.S. 89, 84 S.Ct. 223 (1964).
As *Beck* quoted above clearly demonstrates, this court must weigh the reasons for the arrest with great care. This court must be able to separate the information that the officer had at the time of the arrest with what he learned after the arrest. To allow the state to blur the lines between the two will render the term *probable cause* meaningless.

It is always important to point out to the court that if the court would not have issued a warrant for arrest had the police requested one, then probable cause did not exist.

Whether or not the requirements of reliability and particularity of the information on which an officer may act are more stringent where an arrest warrant is absent, they surely cannot be less stringent than where an arrest warrant is obtained. Otherwise, a principal incentive now existing for the procurement of arrest warrants would be destroyed. *Wong Sun v. United States*, 371 U.S. 471, 83 S.Ct. 407, 9 L.Ed.2d 441.

This standard exists for the safety and security from government intrusions for all citizens. The court in *Wong Sun* noted that there is a history of use and abuse of the power to arrest and they caution that the relaxation of the probable cause standards would "leave law-abiding citizens at the mercy of the officer's whim or caprice." *Wong Sun, supra*, quoting *Brinegar v. United States*, 338 U.S. 160, 176, 69 S.Ct. 1302, 1311, 93 L.Ed. 1879.

A warrantless investigative detention is only lawful if the officer is "able to point to specific and articulable facts which, taken together with rational inferences from those facts, reasonably warrant...[the officer's] intrusion" upon the person's Fourth Amendment rights. *Terry v. Ohio*, 392 U.S. 1, 21, 88 S.Ct. 1868, 1880, 20 L.Ed.2d 889, 906 (1968). Like many reasonable suspicion motions, many probable cause motions have been won by the defense when the State's witnesses simply testify to "signs and symptoms" of impairment and do not describe the actual signs and symptoms individually. Merely stating that there were "signs and symptoms" of impairment are not "specific and articulable facts" from which a court can determine if the officer acted reasonably.

Whether an officer's conduct was "reasonable" or "appropriate" depends on the facts and circumstances of the particular case, so that the decision in one case seldom furnishes a pat answer in another case. (Cites omitted.) A principle to be applied generally however is that in judging the reasonableness of the actions of the officer the circumstances before him are not to be dissected and viewed singly; rather they must be considered as a whole. So considered they are to be viewed through the eyes of a reasonable and cautious officer on the scene, guided by his experience and training. See *United States v. Davis,* 147 U.S.App.D.C. 400, 458 F.2d 819 (1972). *United States v. Hall*, 174 U.S.App.D.C. 13, 15, 525 F.2d 857, 859 (1976).

The Supreme Court of the United States in *Pennsylvania v. Mimms*, 434 U.S. 106, 108-09, 98 S.Ct. 330, 332, 54 L.Ed.2d 331, 335-36 (1977), set forth the test for Fourth Amendment violations in this fashion:

> "The touchstone of our analysis under the Fourth Amendment is always 'the reasonableness in all the circumstances of the particular governmental invasion of a citizen's personal security.' *Terry v. Ohio*, 392 U.S. 1, 19, 88 S.Ct. 1868, 20 L.Ed.2d 889 (1968). Reasonableness, of course, depends 'on a balance between the public interest, and the individual's right to personal security free from arbitrary interference by law officers.' *United States v. Brignoni-Ponce*, 422 U.S. 873, 878, 95 S.Ct. 2574, 45 L.Ed.2d 607 (1975)."

While an arrest definitely occurs with the use of physical restraint, an arrest certainly may occur without physical restraint by the police or even the *magic words "You're under arrest"* being uttered. The varied forms of arrest without physical restraint or an express statement are documented as follows:

United States v. Morrison, 546 F.2d 319, 320 (9th Cir. 1976) When a police officer commands a person to halt or stop, a seizure has occurred.

United States v. Palmer, 603 F.2d 1281 (8th Cir. 1979) Upon the police seeing a suspect walking down a residential street, but not committing any crime, the action of the officer waving his hand and calling the suspect over to the patrol car was deemed a seizure.

Johnson v. United States, 468 A.2d 1325 (D.C. App. 1983) A police officer ordered the driver of a car to "Halt. Come here. Police Officer." was classified as a seizure of the driver.

United States v. Davis, 94 F.3d 1456 (10th Cir. 1986) Escorting a suspect to a patrol car after ordering him to stop and take his hands out of his pockets was a seizure under the Fourth Amendment.

United States v. Wood, 981 F.2d 536 (D.C. Cir. 1992) Police who ordered a suspect to "Halt right there. Stop." had seized the person for Fourth Amendment purposes.

People v. Boodle, 46 N.Y. 2d 398, 391 N.E. 2d 1329 (1979) The order to "Keep your hands where I can see them" constituted a seizure.

Brown v. Texas, 443 U.S. 47 (1979) The act of officers asking a suspect for ID and an explanation for why he was in a public alleyway amounted to a seizure.

State v. Jones, 283 S.E. 2d 483, (1983) Ordering a suspect to step back from a car with his hands in plain view created a seizure under the Fourth Amendment.

United States v. Bowles, 625 F.2d 526 (5th Cir. 1980) Even where suspicious activity is seen, an illegal seizure may occur. A narcotics agent saw a suspect and other engaged in what he believed to be suspicious activity in an airport. The agent's act of walking by the suspect, identifying himself as a narcotics agent by showing ID, and asking him if he could talk for a moment constituted a seizure.

United States v. Turpin, 920 F.2d 1377 (8th Cir. 1990) A seizure occurred where a narcotics agent with a drug-sniffing dog at his side displayed his badge and requested that the suspect sit down.

United States v. Green, 783 F.2d 1364 (9th Cir. 1986) Police drew their weapons and ordered the suspects to place their hands on the car. Clearly, a seizure occurred.

Commonwealth v. Houle, 35 Mass. App. 474, 622 N.E. 2d 638 (1993) A seizure occurred where a uniformed officer asked a suspect if his name was "Bill," and upon seeing something in the suspect's mouth, the officer ordered that he spit it out.

An arrest can certainly occur where there is a show of force. A seizure justified under the *Terry* standards can soon become a full-blown arrest requiring probable cause when the seizure is other than momentary. For instance, when the accused is ordered to halt and lie face down, on the street, this conduct amounts to an arrest and not a temporary detention, *United States v. Delgadill-Velasquez*, 856 F.2d 1292 (9th Cir. 1988). *United States v. Del Vizo*, 918 F.2d 821 (9th Cir. 1990) (Officers stop a vehicle and order for defendants to get out at gunpoint and forced to lie in the street while handcuffed was an arrest).

The passage of time may also convert an investigative detention into an arrest, although there is no black-letter law on what that amount of time is in minutes or hours. But the simple fact that the accused believes that he would be detained for a lengthy period of time without freedom to leave can be considered an arrest without actual force being used. See *Florida v. Royer* 460 U.S. 491, 103 S.Ct. 139, 75 L.Ed 2d 229 (1983).

Washington v. Lambert, 98 F.3d 1181 (9th Cir. 1996) (Police action in shining search light into suspect's car, handcuffing occupants and placing them in the back of a patrol car for five to twenty-five minutes amounted to an arrest).

The fruits of the illegal search must be suppressed. Thus, the correct remedy for a court is to suppress all evidence once it has determined that an illegal search has been made. Where a person has been seized unlawfully, an incidental search is also unlawful and fruits of the search are admissible and cannot be used against the person. *Wong Sun v. United States*, supra.

Motion to Suppress Statements Taken in Violation of Miranda Rights

It is the State's burden to show that Miranda Rights were properly given, that they were understood, and that they were knowingly, voluntarily and intelligently waived before statements may be admitted as evidence. Thus, upon a simple request by the defendant, the State must make such a showing before they can use any statements. One important strategy that should be employed by the defense is to use the probable cause argument above to shift the time of arrest to an earlier point in the investigation prior to the reading of Miranda Rights. The idea is simple: the police can conduct a non-custodial interrogation of a suspect without first advising the suspect of Miranda Warnings. If the police read Miranda Warnings, then that must mean that the suspect was in custody. Clearly, the prosecutor will argue that it was an investigatory detention and not a full-blown arrest. It is your attorney's job to convince the judge otherwise.

To satisfy *Miranda v. Arizona*, 384 U.S. 436, 86 S.Ct. 1602, 16 L.Ed.2d 694 (1966), the State must show that a suspect understood his or her rights and intelligently and knowingly relinquished those rights before custodial interrogation began.

The triggering event for Miranda is custodial interrogation. Simply put, if the suspect is not in custody, the police may ask any question that they choose and the answers will likely be admissible. This is one reason that police have such great success in admitting statements made over the telephone. It is common practice for some types of police investigations for the police to call a suspect at home, and ask incriminating questions. It is a difficult prospect to argue that one is in custody when the police call a suspect at home and ask questions about a crime. The routine gathering of background information on a defendant has generally been held not to constitute an interrogation.

Miranda held that a person "deprived of his freedom in any significant way" could not be questioned unless a valid waiver of those rights was obtained after being adequately advised of them. In general, *Miranda* requires that, before custodial interrogation begins, criminal suspects must be advised that they have the right to remain silent, to consult with counsel, and to have counsel appointed if the suspect cannot afford counsel, and that anything they say may be used against them in a court of law. *Miranda v. Arizona*, 384 U.S. 436, at 444, 86 S.Ct. 1602, at 1612, 16 L.Ed.2d 694 (1966).

Miranda warnings are a prophylactic measure, required at the outset of custodial interrogation, to prevent the state from extracting involuntary confessions from a criminal suspect. *Miranda*, 384 U.S. at 444, 86 S.Ct. at 1612. *Miranda* applies to "questioning initiated by law enforcement officers after a person has been taken into custody or otherwise deprived of his freedom of action in any significant way."

Just like probable cause, one test is to determine if a reasonable person would have felt free to leave. When deciding if an arrest occurred, a significant consideration is the extent to which freedom of movement is curtailed and the degree and manner of force used. *United States v. Beck*, 598 F.2d 497 (9th Circuit 1979). Another significant factor is the display of official authority such that a reasonable person would have believed he was not free to leave.

Motion to Suppress Involuntarily Made Statements

This is an objection to the use of any statements at trial by the State without a ruling on the voluntariness of the statements. Statements made by a defendant are prima facie involuntary. *Jackson v. Denno*, 378 U.S. 368, 84 S.Ct. 1774, 12 L.Ed.2d 908 (1964). The burden is always on the state to show that statements by a defendant were voluntary, and therefore admissible, when the defendant moves for their suppression or objects to their admission. Sometimes it is not wise to move for a voluntariness hearing as in the case where you made good statements to the police. Only your attorney can tell whether this motion should be filed, but remember, your attorney will rely upon you as a major source of information about what you may have said to the police. The police do not always write down everything that you say in their police reports and suddenly "regain" their memories on the stand with a devastating statement.

It is reversible error for a court not to make a ruling on voluntariness when statements are objected to by the defense. More than forty years ago the United States Supreme Court held that before confession can be admitted into evidence, the trial judge must hold a hearing outside the presence of the jury and make a clear finding of voluntariness. *Jackson v. Denno*, 378 U.S. 368, 84 S.Ct. 1774, 12 L.Ed.2d 908 (1964).

Motion to Dismiss Charges for Violation of the Right to Counsel

Unlike Reasonable Suspicion, Probable Cause, Miranda, and Voluntariness motions, a Motion to Dismiss for Violation of the Right to Counsel must affirmatively state the facts of the violation and the defendant has the burden of showing such a violation. This can be done with video or audio tape of the investigation, through the State's own witnesses, or by putting on defense witnesses at a hearing.

In the DUI context, the denial of the right to counsel is a denial of an adequate defense. This is because we can never know what advice an attorney would have given to a suspect by the side of the road. In some states, violation of the right to counsel may lead to the suppression of some evidence. In other states, it can lead to the dismissal of the DUI charges. It is always important to tell your attorney if you asked for an attorney at any point during the investigation.

Violation of the Right to Independent Test

It is important to understand the definition of an independent test. When blood is drawn during a DUI investigation, the police are likely to draw two tubes on blood. One tube is for police testing and the other is for testing by the defense, should the defense choose to do so. This is not an independent test. The second tube (sometimes known as a "split") is for referee testing or secondary testing. An independent test is one with a separate needle stick done by the phlebotomist of the suspect's choosing. The blood will be handled and tested by the people chosen by the defense. For example, the State's blood draw may be contaminated by the method of the draw itself. This would cause problems with either or both tubes of blood drawn by the State. In this respect, the only meaningful sample to the accused would be an independent blood draw with a separate venipuncture and draw.

Independent evidence of sobriety is anything that the accused feels may help him defeat the State's accusations. It could include breath analysis, an examination by a physician of his own choosing, or an independent HGN exam by an ophthalmologist. The list of evidence that could be gathered is quite large and varied, but it is only useful if gathered at a time near the incident.

The idea here is that the defense should have a fair chance to gather independent evidence of sobriety which may be used to counter the state's evidence. This has to be done within a reasonable amount of time after the arrest so that the alcohol would not have a chance to dissipate. In other words, independent evidence of sobriety would be useless if it is gathered 24 hours after the arrest. The police obviously do not want suspects gathering independent evidence of sobriety. It tends to weaken their case against you. The police will often use delay and scare tactics to violate your right to gather exculpatory evidence. This is why it is important to ask for an independent test and to tell your attorney every detail about the arrest and investigation. In some states, the denial of the right to an independent test may lead to suppression of some evidence and in other states it might lead to a dismissal of the DUI charges.

C. Motions in Limine

Motions in Limine are motions filed just before the trial begins. Some motions are routinely granted and others are routinely denied. So, what's the reason for the defense attorney to file motions that will be routinely granted or denied? There are several good reasons.

Routinely granted motions simply put the state on notice of certain aspects of the trial. For example, the state may not comment on the defendant's failure to testify at trial. Everyone knows this and it is well-settled law. However, if the prosecutor makes a bonehead mistake and violates this well-known rule, the defense attorney has the added benefit of being able to point to the motion in limine that was right before trial started and then to accuse the prosecutor of intentional or reckless misconduct. This may make the difference between a mistrial and retrial and a mistrial and dismissal.

6.6 Pretrial Hearings

Pretrial hearings may be held for many reasons. Sometimes they are simple scheduling conferences. Other times they are to determine the outcome of defense and state's motions. Whether you have to attend or not is dependent upon local rules and your attorney's advice. The primary purpose of the pretrial *evidentiary* hearing is to win the motions to suppress and/or dismiss. However, the great collateral benefit is that the defense has the opportunity to cross examine the State's witnesses under oath and on the record. Think of the evidentiary hearing as being able to play poker where you get to see your opponent's hand without showing your own cards. Unless there is some compelling reason (such as in a motion to dismiss for violation of right to counsel), your attorney will likely not have you testify. Circumstances vary from case-to-case. However, rest assured that no one can ever force you to take the stand at any time in any criminal case.

At most pretrial evidentiary hearings one or more of the police who investigated the case will have to testify. This is a fantastic opportunity for the defense to assess the state's witnesses. It is always important for a defendant to take notes and listen to every detail of the police testimony. If you pay careful attention, you may be able to point out exactly where the officer's testimony deviates from the truth. No matter how much your attorney investigates the case, you were the one who was there and your memory of the events is very important to your defense. You can never be too-detailed when recounting the events of the arrest to your attorney.

Note that hearsay is usually admissible at an evidentiary hearing because the court is interested in finding out what the police knew, and when they knew it. Hearsay is an out of court statement, repeated again in court and used to prove the truth of the matter asserted in the statement. Hearsay is inadmissible at trial, with several exceptions. An evidentiary hearing will, generally, be less formal than a trial. However, this does not mean that you should ignore the rules for how to dress and act in court.

6.7 Trial

Whether you get a jury trial or a bench trial (one tried to a judge) will depend on where you were arrested for DUI and how serious the offense is classified. For example, in Nevada one does not have the right to a trial by jury on a misdemeanor DUI. In Washington, one has the right to a trial by a jury of six people. In California, misdemeanor DUIs are tried by a jury of twelve. In any event, the order of the trial is the same with few exceptions.

Courtroom Set-up

The first thing that will take place in a jury trial is jury selection. Generally, more jurors than are needed to sit on the jury are called in for *Voir Dire*. Voir Dire is the legal phrase (taken from the Latin and Middle-French) for the point in the trial where the prospective jurors are questioned about their attitudes and predilections. In some jurisdictions such as Texas, the attorneys are given wide latitude to ask many detailed questions of each juror. In other jurisdictions, the attorneys sit quietly while the judge asks questions off of a script. There is even wide variation within jurisdictions. The important thing for the defense attorney is to listen to the answers and rate the jurors on a scale of acceptability. For the accused, it is important to let your attorney know your input. Many times I have had a client notice something important about a juror that I missed. You are an extra set of eyes and ears for your attorney and this is one of the most critical parts of the trial. Use a notepad to remember the important traits of the potential jurors. Bring these to the attention of your attorney, but remember, your attorney is the one who makes the ultimate determination as to whether to object to a particular juror or not.

After the jury panel is seated and sworn in, the judge should give them some instructions. The instructions usually refer to the juror's conduct during the trial and breaks as well as instructions as to how the trial will proceed and what they are supposed to do during the trial. In virtually all jurisdictions jurors are not allowed to ask questions of the witnesses. In a very few jurisdictions, however, jurors are allowed to ask questions of the witnesses. This is done in writing and the juror questions are subject to the same rules of admissibility as are the attorney's questions.

Opening statements are made. The prosecution goes first and lays out its case for the jury. Prosecutors usually refer to the DUI as a case about choices—the choice to drink and then get behind the wheel. Sometimes I think that they all have the same script to read from, whether the trial is in Maine or Southern California.

Next, the defense makes an opening statement, if the defense chooses to do so. Remember that since the state must prove every element of every charge by proof beyond every reasonable doubt with no help from the defense, the defense does not have to say a word at trial. Typically, however, the defense will make an opening statement right after the prosecution. In rare cases, the defense attorney will reserve opening for the beginning of the defense case. There are many studies which show that jurors make up their minds during opening statements which means that it is wise to make the opening right away. However, you should always trust your attorney's strategy and there may be a very good reason for reserving opening.

The state will call its witnesses first. They question their witnesses in what's called "Direct Examination" where they ask open-ended questions. Leading questions are generally not allowed on direct examination. Next, the defense will have the opportunity to Cross Examine the witness. Cross examination commonly uses leading questions (questions that suggest the answer), but may also employ open-ended questions. My predilection for cross examination is forty-five minutes of my testimony occasionally interrupted by the state's witness agreeing with me.

After cross examination, the state will have the opportunity to do re-direct examination in order to rebut any questions brought up on cross examination. Generally, the examination of the witnesses ends there, however some courts will allow re-cross examination on subjects only brought up on re-direct examination. A very few courts will allow seemingly unending examination of the witnesses until both sides have exhausted every last ounce of energy from the witnesses and the jury is bored to tears.

After the state has subjected all of their witnesses to examination, the state will rest. It is at this point that the defense should raise the question of dismissal to the judge. While the reasons for dismissal vary as much as each case and the standards used by the courts can vary significantly from jurisdiction to jurisdiction, the reason for the dismissal request has the same basis: the state failed in its attempt to prove their case. This is very similar to Summary Judgment in a civil case. Basically, no matter how you slice it, there has been nothing presented which would allow a jury to reach a verdict of guilty. If the judge agrees, then the case is over and an acquittal is entered into the record. If not, then the court moves on to the defense case. Note that where there is more than one charge filed, each charge is subject to a dismissal at this point. In a DUI case, the most common granting of the defense request to dismiss occurs where the state has failed to admit a blood alcohol result. The charges of being over the limit (per se) should be dismissed, but the impairment DUI charge may remain and be decided by the jury.

The defense may choose to out on a case or not after the state rests. The same rules apply, but it is the defense that does direct examination and the state that does cross examination. Typically, the defense case will have an expert witness who is employed to show that the state's tests and investigation were done improperly, or that there is so much variation in the possible results, that there is reasonable doubt.

The defense may also call doctors and other health care workers to testify as to a defendant's medical conditions which would render field sobriety tests or chemical tests unreliable. The defense may also call witnesses who saw the events of the arrest unfold.

The defense can call the accused to the stand. I have always found this risky. Unlike the police and expert witnesses, the client is not a professional witness. Even a poor prosecutor may make it seem as if the client is lying when the client is telling the absolute truth. Whether to take the stand or not is a decision that is wholly within the control of the client. An attorney may neither prevent a client from taking the stand nor force the client to take the stand. The state may not call the accused to the stand and may not comment on the accused's right to remain silent at trial.

Once the defense has rested, in some jurisdictions the state may call rebuttal witnesses to refute the evidence put forth by the defense.

Upon completion of the testimony of all witnesses and the admission of all exhibits, the court will allow closing arguments. In most jurisdictions the prosecution goes first, the defense gives a closing argument and then the prosecution gets one last chance to rebut the defense closing argument. In a minority of jurisdictions, however, the defense goes first and then the prosecution gives a closing argument, but there is no rebuttal testimony.

The jury receives instructions from the judge as to what the law is and how the burden of proof works and they deliberate. The jury may see any admitted exhibit, but they are not allowed to have a transcript of testimony. They must rely upon their memories or notes taken during the trial. (Although in some jurisdictions, jurors may ask to have portions of the testimony read back to them from the record.) They also must not communicate with anyone outside of the jury or do their own research. As cell phones become more adapted to the Internet, more problems arise with jurors doing their own research from the confine of the jury room. Jurors have been know to look at the criminal history of the defendant on line, or check out the many web sites devoted to HGN and filed sobriety testing. All of this is highly improper and should result in a mistrial and retrial.

6.8 Sentencing

Hopefully, you will never have to face sentencing in a DUI case. But if you do, the following information may help. The important thing to remember is that most states have mandatory sentencing laws that take into account BAC and prior offenses. Arizona stands out in the nation as having the most draconian mandatory sentencing laws. A first-time offense will require twenty-four hours in jail. If your BAC is above .15, it will be thirty days in jail. If it is above .20 it is a mandatory minimum of forty-five consecutive days. These are all for first-time offenses. Compare that with Louisiana which has no mandatory jail time.

The most important thing that you can do at the time of sentencing is to listen to your attorney. He or she will know the court system and judge better than you do and can guide you to making the appropriate statements to the court and getting the appropriate substance abuse evaluations and classes done. Your attorney may also ask you not to speak at the time of sentencing because you might compromise your chances on appeal.

A. Mitigation

One can simultaneously prepare for war and peace. Remember that while you and your attorney are planning to win, you must also prepare for loss. One thing to consider is counseling prior to the case coming to trial. In some jurisdictions this will not make a difference in terms of the sentence; in others it may mean the difference between jail time and no jail time. Be sure, however, that if you are in a state which requires counseling upon conviction, the counseling that you do prior to conviction will count. Some states require that a state-licensed substance-abuse counselor be the person to do the counseling. In any event, this is something that you should discuss with your attorney at the first meeting.

If you attend Alcoholics Anonymous meetings, keep track of the AA meetings in a notebook. The notebook should contain the date and time of the meeting, the group name for the particular meeting, location and have a signature from the group leader, acknowledging that you were present. When it comes time for sentencing, the notebook will be very helpful in mitigation.

B. Substance Abuse Counseling

In general, one of two types of assessments will be given to someone who is convicted of DUI and is referred for counseling. The assessments are used to determine what level of counseling is appropriate; however, as virtually every DUI defense practitioner has seen, if the case involves a particularly high BAC, the results of the assessment are ignored and the person is assigned to the highest level of counseling available.

One of the assessments given is known as the MAST (Michigan Alcoholism Screening Test). It is a 25-question Yes/No assessment administered by another person (i.e. not self-assessment). Answers are weighted according to importance. If one scores 5 or higher, alcoholism is highly suspected. The MAST test virtually assures that everyone who takes it as a result of a court order or on the advice of an attorney is labeled as an alcoholic. For example, having attended one AA meeting nets five points. Having been arrested for DUI nets 2 points.

Thus, anyone who has been arrested for DUI and has attended an AA meeting at the request of an attorney or by order of the court scores 7 points and is labeled an alcoholic.

Another test given is the SASSI© (Substance Abuse Subtle Screening Inventory). The SASSI-3© is for adults 18 and over, with a reading grade level slightly above 3rd grade, and takes about 15 minutes to administer. It uses 65 True/False questions. It too contains questions that will hurt anyone assigned to counseling as the result of a DUI conviction. For example, one True/False question is "I have sometimes drunk too much." Clearly, if you have been convicted of a DUI, you might feel that even one drink was too much. Another True/False question is: "When I drink and use drugs I tend to get into trouble." How does one answer that question if one does not use drugs at all? If you answer "false," does that mean that you drink and use drugs, but get away with it?

There are other assessments used by various jurisdictions. None of them have the ability to accurately diagnose and suggest proper treatment. They are simply a "feel-good" requirement by the courts to make the public and legislatures think that they are having an effect on behavior.

C. Home-Monitoring

Home monitoring is a valuable alternative to jail time where allowed. Home monitoring will require approval of the court, usually gained by a court-staff member or probation monitor visiting the home to assess the appropriateness of the setting. Alcohol generally will not be allowed in the home during the period of home monitoring. It will often require a telephone landline and the deactivation of call-waiting and other features. If you are still living in the 90s and have dial-up Internet access, you must have a second line installed.

Home monitoring requires an ankle-bracelet and a device hooked up to the phone line. Like an invisible fence for dogs, you cannot wander off. If you stray too far from the monitoring device hooked up to the telephone, the telephone device will call the monitoring company who will, in turn, notify the probation department that you have escaped.

At regularly scheduled intervals, you may be free to leave home for work or school. Generally, upon arrival back, you must call the monitoring company.

The monitoring company will call you at regular and random intervals and have you activate a small button on the ankle monitor. The telephone device may be equipped with a breath tester for random or regular use. The device will have photo-capture capability which will allow the monitor to confirm that the person blowing into the machine is actually you.

Home monitoring charges will generally be charged to you but they can be significantly less expensive than the costs of incarceration.

D. Secure Continuous Real-time Alcohol Monitoring (SCRAM)

SCRAM ankle devices seem to be all the rage now that celebrities are seen wearing them. A SCRAM device attaches to your ankle and continuously monitors alcohol emitted in your perspiration. The device cannot be removed and if you try to slip something between the device and your leg, it should recognize the tampering and flag it as such. They are connected wirelessly to a device which transmits the data to a monitoring company.

Fortunately, the devices are getting smaller as technology advances and they provide a much better alternative to sitting in a jail cell. Yet many states will not accept them as an alternative to incarceration.

E. Ignition Interlock Devices

An ignition interlock device (IID) is a breath-testing machine which will prevent the driver from starting the car if he has a BAC at or above a certain level. Many interlock devices have as "rolling retest" which requires the driver to provide another sample of breath at some point after the car has been started. This prevents a person from starting the car and leaving it running while drinking. Most often, the IID is leased from a certified provider and installed at the car owner's expense. They can be checked at regular intervals and a record of breath test results disclosed to a probation department or to the court.

IIDs are becoming more popular with the courts as MADD pushes state legislators to pass mandatory ignition interlock laws for first-time offenders. It is the ultimate goal of MADD to see all new cars equipped with such devices. There is no credible research that shows that mandatory IID orders reduce drunk driving.

F. Letters to the Judge

Any letters to the judge on behalf of you need to be screened by your attorney before they are sent to the judge. Typically, the best way to do this is to gather letters from all those people who are willing to help and give them to your attorney at the same time. The attorney will screen them for content, spelling, grammar, and be sure that they have the judge's name right. If they are not perfect, they should be sent back with instructions as to how to correct them or not submitted at all.

Each letter writer should be given an outline. The outline should contain the following points:

- Name of the letter writer.
- Relationship to you.
- Short statement of your good points.
- Acknowledgment of the seriousness of the crime.
- A statement of willingness to help you get back on track.

The letter to the judge is not a forum for the writers to dispute the charges or badmouth the prosecutor, police, witnesses or court system. If the letter-writer feels poorly toward any of them, he should keep it to himself. The writer also should not try to explain, or even mention, other bad acts you committed. For example, if you have many out-of-wedlock children that you must care for, now is not the time to mention it. The judge may get the feeling of a general lack of responsibility on your part. The letters should only emphasize the good points, not explain the bad points.

6.9 Plea Bargains

DUI plea offers are different in many respects than other plea offers. In the DUI area, many prosecutors' hands are tied by mandatory sentencing laws, legislation which requires prosecution, as well as their own office policies.

DUI is not a political crime, but it is a highly politicized crime. Chief prosecutors are elected and appointed using the same "Get Tough on Crime" message, not a "Let's Do Justice" message. Since DUI is so highly politicized and blown out of proportion, it is easy for a would-be Chief Prosecutor to campaign on the promise of no plea bargaining in DUI cases. Yet, anyone who practices in this area knows that they have to offer plea bargains in order to function. If every defense attorney set every DUI case for trial, the system would collapse.

As a result, we find that many plea offers are made which ask a defendant to plead guilty or no contest, receive the bare minimum sentence, and all civil traffic charges will be dismissed. Sometimes we find plea offers which will drop a high per se BAC charge if the accused pleads to the underlying DUI or BAC charge.

When deciding whether or not to take a plea offer, your attorney should not push you into a decision. That's not to say, however, that your attorney should withhold advice. Remember that you have retained your attorney not only for his or her legal skills, but also because the attorney has some experience in these types of situations. There are times when you should reject the plea offer because there is a strong defense case. There are other times when you will be slaughtered at trial and you are only playing for the fumble. Remember, in either situation and in all of the situations in between, it is you, not your attorney, who will have to live with the conviction should you plea or take the matter to trial and lose. Your attorney must fully inform you of all of the ramifications of the decision. Putting it in writing is a very good method.

A. Guilty vs. No Contest

In simple terms, a plea of "Guilty" means that you admit to all of the facts alleged in the plea offer. A plea of "No Contest" means that you agree that if there were a trial, you would lose, but you do not admit to the facts involved. Either way, the judge finds you guilty.

The advantage to a No Contest plea is that if there is a civil suit arising out of the incident (such as where there is an accident), you will not have admitted to the facts, which will then have to be proven at a civil trial. There is no advantage to a No Contest plea over a Guilty plea where there is no possibility of a civil action arising out of the incident.

B. Waiver of Rights

You must always be informed of your waiver of rights prior to taking a plea. Most judges do it properly, but some do not. In either event, a competent attorney always advises the client of the rights waived prior to ever entering the courtroom to accept a plea offer. This should be done in writing by your attorney as well as in a face-to-face discussion. A good practice is for your attorney to write a letter to you which explains the rights, then sit with you and go over each right, line-by-line. Those rights are:

- The right to a trial (by jury in some jurisdictions).
- The right to confront and cross examine witnesses for the State.
- The right to compel favorable witnesses by subpoena to testify.
- The right to remain silent and have the State prove each element of every charge.
- The right to a direct appeal.
- The right to counsel, should you not be able to afford an attorney.

Most judges will ask if the accused has had any alcohol or drugs during the 24 hours preceding the change-of-plea proceeding that would affect their decision. The judge should also inform you that if you are not a U.S. Citizen, a DUI conviction may have immigration consequences.

6.10 Collateral Consequences

As we know, a DUI conviction can have onerous collateral consequences. Be sure to discuss with your attorney the adverse effects on immigration, professional licenses, security clearances, military discipline, auto insurance, health insurance, license loss, commercial driver status, ignition interlock requirements and the like.

6.11 Exposure of Prior Offenses

Read the plea offer carefully before you accept it, especially if you have a prior DUI offense. Often, plea offers carry language that forces the defendant to acknowledge that he has no prior DUI convictions or pending cases and is not on probation for any other offenses at the time of signing the plea offer. Some offers will even go as far as requiring your defense attorney to acknowledge that you have no priors and nothing pending. Sometimes the prosecution does not know about a prior offense, but you and your attorney do.

If the attorney knows of a prior offense, he or she cannot sign a plea agreement that requires acknowledgment that nothing exists. That would be a clear ethical violation of being honest with the tribunal and fairness to opposing counsel. Asking the prosecutor to strike such language will certainly tip him or her off to the fact that you have a prior offense or something pending. Your attorney has limited choices in this situation.

The first choice is to not enter into the plea and take the matter to trial.

The second choice is not to enter into the plea and plead to the court.

The third choice is to withdraw and let you do as you choose, but this might raise some red flags. Remember that you may not commit perjury and a fraud upon the court.

6.12 Immigration Consequences

A DUI conviction, whether as a result of trial or plea, may affect immigration status of a non-citizen. It could result in the deportation or removal of a person from this country. It could prevent you from ever gaining legal status in the United States or becoming a citizen. Each case is as different as each person's status. Be sure to tell your attorney if you are not a United States citizen. You may want to consult with an attorney who is knowledgeable in the immigration area.

A misdemeanor DUI conviction will also be a bar to entry of non-Canadian citizens who wish to visit Canada.

6.13 Appeals

An appeal is taken after a verdict and is covered by strict local rules. Generally, an appeal must be taken within a specific period of time after entry of judgement and sentencing. More often than not, if an appellate deadline is missed, the right to appeal is extinguished forever. In a minority of cases the appeal is taken after the deadline, but upon the discovery of new evidence which could not have been discovered through due diligence on the part of the defense prior to trial. Fortunately, the prosecution cannot appeal from a not guilty verdict.

Appeals are based on a mistake of law or prosecutorial misconduct. Although some court rules allow an appeal to be taken when the verdict is against the weight of the evidence, that type of appeal is likely to fail.

The appellate process generally follows these steps: a Notice of Appeal is filed and the court record is prepared for the appellate court. The Appellant (the party seeking the reversal) writes a brief stating the reasons why the decision should be reversed. The Appellee (the party that won in the trial court) writes a Response stating the reasons why the verdict should stand. The Appellant may, but is not required to, file a Reply to the Appellee's Response. The Appellate Court reads the briefs and holds oral argument on the Appeal. It is important to realize that the Appeal is based on the record from the trial court. If the issue was not raised in the lower court, then it will likely be barred on appeal. No new evidence is taken at the appellate level, except where there is an issue of newly discovered evidence.

6.14 Expungement

Expungement is the erasure of a criminal record. It is not available in all states. In some states, you can have your record "sealed" which means that someone may find out that you have a criminal record, but not be able to find out what the charges were or how they were decided. Sealing a record is not the best idea because someone can see that there was a criminal proceeding, but not the charge. The person might jump to the wrong conclusion and assume that it was child molestation and not DUI.

In addition to a criminal record, there will also be a Department of Motor Vehicles record. This record is often subject to completely different record-keeping rules than a criminal record. It may do you no good to expunge a criminal record, yet leave the motor vehicle record untouched.

Be wary of private databases. With the increase of the use of the Internet, there are companies that keep private records of criminal and motor vehicle records. Insurance companies keep their own records as do credit reporting agencies. There may be little or nothing that you can do to expunge these records.

Chapter 7

Blood Alcohol Calculations

7.1 Chapter Overview

Entire books have been devoted to blood alcohol calculations in humans. This chapter is not designed as a treatise on the disposition of alcohol in humans or as a reference for expert witnesses. Many formulae exist for the determination of BAC in humans. Most require conversion of Metric to English measurements. Some require the Body Mass Index (BMI) of the subject. All are complex.

This chapter is designed for people who simply want to know how to calculate quickly the approximate BAC numbers for themselves and others based on what has been consumed. Please note that the results are for *approximate* BAC calculations. Physiological conditions, stomach contents, elimination rates and other factors will change the result.

DO NOT RELY ON THE CALCULATIONS TO DETERMINE WHAT YOU CAN SAFELY DRINK BEFORE DRIVING!

7.2 Determining the One-Drink Potential

A *one-drink potential* is the maximum BAC that a person will reach after one drink. It is very simple to do: you only need four pieces of information and a calculator:

1. Subject's gender (males use .13; females use .11)
2. Subject's body weight in pounds
3. Type of drink (or alcohol content)
4. Size of drink in ounces

For example, the calculations for a 180 pound male who was drinking 12-ounce, 4.16% alcohol, beers are as follows:

$$\frac{(12 \text{ oz. beer})(.0416 \text{ alcohol content})}{(180 \text{ lbs.})(.13 \male)} = \frac{.499}{23.4} = .021 \text{ per drink}$$

The man has a one-drink potential of .021. In other words, .021 is the maximum BAC that he would reach after consuming one drink.

If this man has four Bud Lights, the maximum his BAC could be would be .021 × 4 or .084. This does not account for elimination.

Men and women are different in so many ways, it is not surprising that they are also different in their one-drink potential. This is due to the fact that, on average, women have a higher body fat to water ratio than men. Although on average most women are shorter and lighter than most men, women tend to carry more fat in their breasts, buttocks and thighs than men. Clearly this may be reversed in some instances such as when we compare a very physically fit woman with an obese man, but the generalizations made here hold true enough for these estimations.

Take the same facts as above, but change the gender from male to female and we find a different one-drink potential:

$$\frac{(12 \text{ oz. beer})(.0416 \text{ alcohol content})}{(180 \text{ lbs.})(.11 \female)} = \frac{.499}{19.8} = .025 \text{ per drink}$$

If this woman has four Bud Lights, the maximum her BAC could be would be .025 × 4 or .100. This, too, does not account for elimination.

The gender difference is embodied in Widmark's rho factor. Widmark's rho factor is a mathematical expression of the ratio of body fat to water in men and women. The rho factor has been moved from the numerator of Widmark's formula into the denominator of the formula above. For men, use .13; for women, use .11.

When figuring alcohol content for drinks that express alcohol content in terms of *proof*, simply divide the proof in half. Thus, 80-proof vodka has 40% alcohol. Sometimes proof is expressed as a small circle similar to a degree sign used for temperature. For example, "80 proof" can also be expressed as "80°".

7.3 Elimination and Retrograde Extrapolation

When attorneys discuss elimination, they are mainly discussing the metabolization of the alcohol by the body, rather than the actual elimination of alcohol from the body.

A very small amount of alcohol leaves the body in an unchanged state (less than 6%). Most alcohol is metabolized by enzymes in the *alcohol dehydrogenase pathway.* Alcohol dehydrogenase, aldehyde dehydrogenase, acetaldehyde and other enzymes play a part in the biological oxidation of alcohol and its metabolites. One can trace the path of alcohol elimination on a molecular level in great detail. My belief is that juries are bored by this, judges are confused by it and prosecutors don't know what to do with it on cross-examination.

What we need to know is that after alcohol has been consumed, it is eliminated at a relatively steady rate; rates of elimination have been recorded as low as .008 per hour and as high as about .035 per hour. Generally, alcoholics and binge drinkers with high BACs eliminate faster than inexperienced drinkers. The average rate accepted by most forensic toxicologists is .010 to .017 per hour, depending on whom you talk to. It is not gender dependant like absorption is.

This means that a man with a .100 BAC will be a .000 BAC in ten hours if the elimination rate is .010 per hour. Eliminating .010 per hour from his known BAC is a *retrograde extrapolation* (sometimes known as back extrapolation). If the same man has an elimination rate of .015 per hour, he will be a .000 in less than seven hours. A retrograde extrapolation is nothing more than choosing an hourly elimination rate and subtracting that amount from the known BAC. The one caveat to a retrograde extrapolation is that the person must be in the elimination phase of alcohol consumption.

7.4 White's Retrograde Extrapolation

A White's retrograde extrapolation calculates the number of drinks that need to be unabsorbed in the subject's stomach in order for the subject to be under the legal limit at the time of driving. This is also known as a "rising BAC" defense. Some states have eliminated the rising BAC defense and, instead, rely on the BAC at the time of the chemical test. While this defies all logic, it is the law in some jurisdictions.

Yet, even in states that have eliminated the rising BAC defense, the White's retrograde extrapolation is still important in the scenario where your defense rests not on the particular BAC within two hours of driving, but on lack of impairment at the time of driving, such as in an endangerment case.

Take, for example, the scenario where a person is charged with two counts of endangerment after rear-ending a car with two passengers at a stoplight. The accident was at 2:15 A.M. His BAC was measured just a half hour after the accident at 2:45 A.M., and it was .090. If he downed his last drink when the bar closed at 2:00 A.M., some of the alcohol could have been unabsorbed at the time of the accident but fully absorbed at the time of the breath test.

If he is the 180-pound man from the one-drink potential example, the value of the 12-ounce beer could be subtracted from his reported BAC. Thus, we subtract .021 from .090, and the result is a .069. Because we don't know how fast he actually absorbed that 12-ounce beer into his bloodstream, he could have been anywhere from a .069 to the reported result of .090. Under these facts, a defense attorney will never prove that his client was under the limit, but the state will never prove that he was over the limit, either.

The White's retrograde formula can be expressed as follows:

$$\frac{\text{test result} + \left\{\left[(\text{elapsed time*}) \times (\text{elimination rate a})\right] - (.079)\right\}}{(\text{one} - \text{drink potential})}$$

$$= \text{number of drinks unabsorbed in stomach}$$

* Elapsed Time from time of last drink to time of chemical test.

a Choose the elimination rate within human limitations that suits your purpose.

$$\frac{(.090) + \left\{\left[(.75\ \text{hours})(.010/\text{hr})\right] - (.079)\right\}}{(.021)} = \frac{(.098) - (.079)}{(.021)} =$$

$$= 0.88\ \text{drinks}$$

$$(0.88\ \text{drinks}) \times (12\ \text{oz. drink size}) = 10.6\ \text{oz.}$$

This means that if he had 0.88 drinks (or 10.6 oz.) unabsorbed in his stomach at the time of the accident, he was no higher than a .079.

Chapter 8

Choosing an Attorney

8.1 Chapter Overview

Self-representation, finding an attorney, attorney interviews, attorney-client privacy and fees are discussed in this chapter. Many people are apprehensive about meeting with an attorney. Knowing what to expect and what questions to ask can alleviate much of that apprehension. Fees vary greatly depending upon the area of the country, court process, complexity of the case and the severity of the charge. There is no real guide to what a "good deal" may be since fees can legitimately vary from $2,000 to $12,000 or more for the same charge and in the same jurisdiction.

At the end of this chapter you will find a checklist of common issues surrounding a DUI case. Read the checklist over and make notes of the things that apply to your case. Be prepared to discuss the issues with attorneys that you consult.

8.2 Should I Represent Myself?

No. Even if you are an attorney, you should not represent yourself. A DUI, whether it be a felony or a misdemeanor, is the most complex of all criminal cases. It requires a thorough knowledge of Fourth, Fifth and Sixth Amendment Constitutional Law, State Constitutional Law, Administrative Law, and State Statutes. The Rules of Evidence are complex and are influenced by both federal and state case law. The Rules of Criminal Procedure require that the case proceed in a specific manner. Oftentimes a misstep in following the rules will mean that your evidence will not be admissible at trial, or that the government's evidence which should have been suppressed will be used to convict you. Most non-attorneys have neither the skill nor the education required to formulate proper questions.

DUI is an opinion crime. In other words, in many states the government's witnesses may render an opinion as to whether the driver is under the influence or impaired. The police investigative techniques are of paramount importance to that opinion. Most people have no clue as to what the police manuals require the police to do during their DUI investigations. Field Sobriety Testing is nothing more than voodoo based on incomplete, inaccurate and unscientific studies. The general public has little idea of what these tests entail and how to defeat them in court.

Science is heavy throughout the entire case. Knowledge of human physiology and pharmacokinetics is important. If the case involves a blood test, you will need to know not only about phlebotomy, but also about headspace gas chromatography. If there is a breath test involved, an intimate knowledge of infrared spectroscopy or fuel cell dynamics is necessary. And, if it is a DUI-drugs case, you will need to understand headspace gas chromatography mass-spectroscopy before you can tackle the case.

8.3 Resources—How Do I Find a DUI Attorney?

DUI is a very specialized area of the law and requires a specialist. However, this does not mean that the entire firm has to do nothing but DUI. Many large firms have attorneys that specialize in one particular area, yet it is rare to see a large firm that does both civil and criminal work who has a dedicated DUI attorney.

Most firms that do DUI work are smaller and will oftentimes not do any civil work. Some firms are so specialized that they do DUI and traffic-related work exclusively. Such firms are easier to find in states that have harsh penalties and strict enforcement of DUI laws. In other states, where the penalties are not very harsh and enforcement is relaxed, it is difficult to make a living specializing in DUI cases.

While you might not want to ask friends and neighbors about DUI attorneys because you are embarrassed to have been arrested, if you know someone close who has had a DUI, you can ask that person for a referral. Also, one of the best referral sources is an attorney with whom you have done business in the past.

One can certainly check the phonebook as well as the Internet for local attorneys, but be careful. Watch out for attorneys who state that they have "successfully handled hundreds of DUI cases" or similar quotes. Just what does "successfully handled" mean? Does it mean that they were all done without a bar complaint? Also be wary of those who advertise that they were former prosecutors. Those people might well know how to put people in jail for DUI, but not have a clue as to how to defend them.

Watch out for the term "specialist" as well. In Arizona, the term "Certified Criminal Law Specialist" means a tremendous amount. It takes hard work, dedication, extra continuing legal education requirements and an exam to become a specialist. In other states, such as California, anyone can call him or herself a specialist.

There is only one nationwide DUI certification recognized by the American Bar Association. It has been offered by the National College for DUI Defense since 2000. Applicants must not only pass a background check, have letters of reference from judges and attorneys, but must also pass a rigorous examination covering virtually all aspects of DUI defense. As of January 2007, there are only thirty-nine Board Certified DUI Defense Attorneys in the country. Board Certification lasts only five years and must be renewed. Look for the term "Board Certified by the National College for DUI Defense" when you are looking for an attorney. Board Certified attorneys can be found at the National College for DUI Defense's website: www.NCDD.com.

A. Attorney Interview

You should make appointments with and interview at least three attorneys before you make your choice. Bring all of your paperwork with you to the interview. This might be as simple as just the ticket, or it might be the complete police report with blood test results. Whatever it is, bring it with you to the interview. The attorney will decide what is important and what is not.

Also, if you were taking any medications on the date that you were arrested, write down the dosage and name of the medication. Make a list of any illness or injuries that you have sustained. Every attorney will want to know about a head injury, no matter how old it is. Keep in mind that diseases of the blood, lungs, and gastro-intestinal problems can have significant effects on breath, blood and urine testing. At the end of this chapter is a checklist of major issues regarding health and other aspects of the DUI investigation that your attorney will be interested in. Read it over and be prepared to discuss the issues when you meet with your attorney.

B. Attorney-Client Relationship

What you tell your attorney is protected by the attorney-client relationship. The attorney may not reveal what has been said without your permission. As with any rule, however, there are exceptions to the confidentiality requirement.

One exception is that the confidential information must actually be given in confidence. This means that if there is another person in the room, who is not a member of the attorney's litigation staff, the information given is not protected. Oftentimes this situation occurs when a parent or spouse of the client is present during the initial consultation. If you are consulting with an attorney about your case and you have someone with you either for moral or financial support, it is perfectly acceptable to have that person present when you are discussing the elements of the criminal laws, possible punishment, fees and the process of the case. But when it comes time to discuss the facts that no one else knows about, such as what, when, where or how much alcohol you might have consumed, then you should ask to speak to the attorney alone. Clearly, this can present an awkward situation when a spouse or family member is present. One of the better ways to present this to your loved one is to explain that if anyone were to find out that someone else was present, then the attorney could be forced to divulge the information.

Another thing to keep in mind is that it doesn't matter who pays the fee. The attorney-client relationship exists between the attorney and the client, not the attorney and the party who pays the fee. This, too can cause some awkward moments. Remember that your attorney will not lie for you, but your attorney will simply refer the party to the attorney-client relationship.

Your attorney will likely tell you not to speak to anyone about the facts of the case. With the exception of speaking to another prospective attorney, this is sound advice. You can easily destroy the confidentiality agreement by shooting off your mouth about the facts of the case. Some people are very private about their affairs and want to keep the DUI accusation as secret as possible. Other people think that every stranger on the bus wants to hear all of the details. For your own sake, do not discuss the case with anyone other than your attorney.

It does not matter whether you actually retain the attorney or not. An initial consultation with an attorney about your case, even where you do not ultimately retain the attorney, is protected by the attorney-client confidentiality rules. Money does not have to change hands for the confidentiality rules to apply.

The attorney may disclose confidential information to a member of the firm, or in some cases, to investigators who are under contract with the firm for a particular case. Clearly this makes sense as the investigator or expert witness may need to evaluate and advise the attorney as to how to proceed with a particular issue. The attorney makes the disclosure decisions based on a need-to know basis and the particular local confidentiality rules.

C. Fees

"Fees should be reasonable." That is a quote found in almost every ethical guideline in every state. But, what is reasonableness based upon?

The reasonableness of a fee can be based on the following:

The attorney's experience in the area. Clearly, a new attorney can be competent to handle your case. But with time and practice the attorney should (hopefully) have run into situations similar to yours and have already formulated a response. Even where there is a brand new issue to be resolved, an attorney with years of experience may be better-equipped to tackle the problem.

The reputation of the attorney factors into the mix as well. Expect to pay more for one of the thirty-nine Board Certified DUI Defense Attorneys in the country. There are attorneys who are well-known as tough, aggressive and smart. Prosecutors know who they are and make better deals with them than with less-aggressive attorneys or who are not as experienced in the area. Should the attorney be able to charge more for his or her reputation? Of course.

The availability of the firm or the attorney may also be a factor. It is perfectly proper for the attorney to assess whether the firm will turn down any cases because they are handling your case. Attorneys lose cases at a higher rate when they start stretching their resources too thin. Any attorney who has been around for a while has seen the attorney who constantly misses court appearances or who is always asking the judge for a continuance of a court date, or for an extension of time to file motions. While there are certainly legitimate reasons for this, the attorneys who do this as a routine practice are stretched too thin and should take less cases. This also suggests that one should not look for the cheapest fee on the market. Attorneys who charge cheap fees may not be able to look after the cases diligently. There is nothing unseemly or improper about charging a client for the true value of the attorney's services. The bottom line with fees is: Expect to get what you pay for.

The attorney's resources are part of the formula to account for reasonableness. Law libraries are not cheap to maintain. There are many resources devoted specifically to DUI defense. A modest in-house law library can cost over $10,000 to purchase, and because criminal and DUI laws change so rapidly, updates and computer database services can easily run over $1,000 per month for a solo practitioner attorney.

The complexity of the case certainly figures into the fee structure. A plain-vanilla-first-time misdemeanor-DUI should cost less than a second-time DUI with an accident. This is a function of the amount of time that will be involved in the case. Felonies will cost more than misdemeanors both because of the time involved and the gravity of the situation.

Out-of-Pocket expenses are often in addition to the fee. Out-of-pocket expenses are generally used for such things as photocopy and transcript expenses. The largest expense is generally for one or more expert witnesses. Experts may be used for accident reconstruction, field sobriety testing, breath testing, blood testing, speech pathology, pharmacokinetics, etc.

A "Contingent Fee" is one where the client does not pay if the attorney does not win. Contingent fees are quite popular in personal injury cases and are usually based on the amount of money recovered from the opposing party. Contingent fees are illegal in criminal cases in every state. If an attorney offers you a contingent fee, run, don't walk away.

Finally, don't be afraid to ask the attorney about payment plans. Some attorneys will require a fee up-front and others will accept payments from clients.

Trades can often be done. I know of several attorneys who have traded legal services for cars as well as for services such as painting and masonry work. Whatever the arrangement is, be sure that you are comfortable with it and that it is in writing.

8.4 Checklist of Issues to Discuss With Your Attorney

The following checklist should be used to help remind you of issues to discuss with your attorney. It is not a substitute for your attorney's intake form or to supplant the strategies and procedures that he or she will employ to defend you.

If you received any paperwork from your arrest, bring it with you to show to your attorney.

A. The Traffic Stop

Describe the roadway where you first encountered the police?
Which direction were you headed?
What lane were you in?
What was the lighting like at the time?
Do you think that the officer saw you leaving a bar parking lot?
How long had you been driving before you were stopped?
Where did you stop and why did you choose that location as opposed to other locations?
Did the officer use lights, siren, or any other method of alerting you to stop?
Why do you think that you were stopped?
Did the officer cite you for any traffic violations?
Did the officer tell you why you were stopped?
Did the officer ask you for any vehicle documents or your license?
Did you produce them?
Did the officer ask you if you had something to drink or taken any drugs?
Did you tell the officer than you had something to drink?
How did the officer ask you to step out of the vehicle?
Did you have any trouble stepping out?
Do you think that this was a case of racial profiling by the police?
If so, why?
Did the officer ever tell you that you were free to go?
Did the officer do or say anything that you felt was inappropriate?

B. Facts of the Investigation and Arrest

Was there a videotape, audio recording or photographs of the investigation?
Were your fingerprints taken at any time?
Was there a booking photo taken?

Was your vehicle searched?
Did they find anything?

Did the officer ask you to do any physical tests?
Did the officer threaten you in any manner or tell you that physical tests were mandatory?
Did the officer explain them to you?
Did the officer demonstrate any portion of the physical tests?
Did the officer ask you any questions about your health or physical disabilities at any point?
Were you removed from the traffic-stop area for testing?

Did the officer ask to look at your eyes, or do an eye test?
Did the officer have you follow a finger or object with your eyes only?
Were you asked to walk on a straight line?
Was a real line used, or was it an imaginary line?
Were you asked to stand on one leg?
Did you do any other physical tests?
Were you asked to write anything?

Did you submit to any chemical test or refuse to take any tests?
If you refused, how did you refuse?
If you refused, did the police administer a chemical test against your will?
Did the police seek or get a search warrant to forcibly draw blood?
Did you recant your refusal?
Did you choose what type of chemical test you took?
Did the police read you any forms regarding chemical testing?

Did you submit to any breath test(s)?
If so, how many breath samples did you provide?
Were you tested on more than one machine?
Did you have any trouble blowing?

Was blood drawn?
How many tubes were drawn?
What was the color of the tops of the tubes?
Did the phlebotomist have any trouble drawing blood?
At what location was your blood drawn (hospital or police station)?
Where was the blood drawn from (arm, hand, other)?

Did the police collect a urine sample from you?

Did the police ever discuss whether you could get an independent test of your blood, breath or urine?

Did the officer inform you of your Miranda Rights?
Did you waive your rights or remain silent?
Did you ask for an attorney?

Were you asked to rate your sobriety on a scale?
Were you asked questions about what, when, where or how much you drank?
Did you tell the officer?

At what point were you handcuffed, if at all?
Did the police tell you that you were under arrest at some point? When?
Did the police impound your vehicle?
When did they tell you it was going to be impounded?

C. The Police Officer(s)

How many police officers were involved in the entire investigation?
What were their names?
Were you treated politely and with respect?
Do you know any of them?

D. Physical Health and Status at the Time of the Traffic Stop

What is the extent of your education?
Is English your first language?

What was your weight at the time of arrest?
Were you dieting? What type of diet were you on?
When did you start drinking?
When was your last drink?
How much did you drink?
What were you drinking?
When was your last meal?
What was it?

Do you have any allergies?
To what?
Do you wear glasses or contacts (or should you wear them)?

Do you have any hearing loss?

Do you have any physical disabilities?
Do you have any prosthesis, artificial joints or implanted medical devices?
Have you had any surgeries? Please list them.

Have you ever had a head injury?
Have you ever been told that you have nystagmus?
Do you have, or have you had any inner-ear problems?
Do you have poor balance?

Did you visit a different time-zone within 72 hours of the DUI arrest?
Do you work odd hours (night shift, graveyard shift)?
How much sleep did you have in the 48 hours prior to the stop?
Do you have insomnia?

Do you have Gastro-Esphogeal Reflux Disease (GERD)?
Do you have frequent heartburn?
Do you have Chronic Obstructive Pulmonary Disease (COPD)?
Do you have diabetes?
Do you have any disease of the blood?
Do you have liver disease?
Were you sick, or not feeling well on the day that you were arrested?
Did you have a fever on that day?

Do you have depression, anxiety, or bi-polar disorders?
Have you ever had any of these?
Have you ever had any mental health issues? What were they? Were you treated?

E. Medications

Were you taking any prescription medications within one month of being arrested?
List the dosage, frequency and reason.

Were you taking any over-the-counter medications within one month of being arrested?
List the dosage, frequency and reason.

Were there any medications prescribed to you that you should have been taking, but were not?

List the dosage, frequency and reason.
Why were you not taking the medication?

F. Witnesses

Were you traveling in a group or two or more cars?
Did the people in the other car witness the driving and police traffic stop of your vehicle?
Write down the names, addresses and phone numbers of all witnesses that you know about and give them to your attorney.

G. Passengers

If there were any passengers in your vehicle at the time of the DUI stop or at an earlier time, your attorney will want to know about them. Those who were in the vehicle earlier may be able to attest to good driving. Write down the names, addresses and phone numbers of all passengers and give them to your attorney. Let your attorney know if any of your passengers were minors—this fact may govern whether certain additional charges are filed such as child abuse or child endangerment.

H. Drivers License Status

What was the status of your drivers license at the time that you were stopped?
If it was invalid, why was it invalid (i.e. unpaid tickets, or a previous DUI)?
Do you have a commercial drivers license?
Do you have any tickets or accidents in the last five years?

I. Prior Criminal History

Do you have any prior DUI arrests or convictions?
If so, when and where?
What were the charges?
What was the disposition of the charges?
Did you tell anyone about a prior conviction or arrest?
Did the police or prosecutor discuss a prior conviction or arrest with you?

J. Collateral Issues

Are you a U.S. citizen?
If not, what is your status?
Do you ever visit Canada?
Do you hold any professional licenses (real estate, nurse, pharmacist)?

Did you pay bail to be released from jail?
How much?
Who posted it?

K. Costs of the Representation

What will the representation cost in terms of legal fees?
What does the fee include?
Does it include trial?
Does it include any drivers license hearings?
Does it include appeals or post-conviction relief?
If my case is dismissed and charges are refiled, will there be additional fees?
In addition to legal fees, are there any out-of-pocket expenses that must be paid for?
What are they for and what are the approximate costs?
Is there a payment plan available?

Index

Notes

Notes

Other quality products available from:

Lawyers & Judges Publishing Company, Inc.

Medical-Legal Aspects of Alcohol, Fourth Edition

edited by James C. Garriott Ph.D.

In the fourth edition of *Medical-Legal Aspects of Alcohol*, we've taken the best of the previous editions and added brand-new content to prepare for you a comprehensive guide to the dense subject of alcohol. The information in this book goes well beyond drinking and driving. It does justice to the broad and complex topic of alcohol. It is written for attorneys, forensic scientists, medical examiners, coroners—any professional who needs information on alcohol's disposition in the body. Editor James Garriott and twenty of the field's leading experts cover all facets of alcohol, with chapters on: defending and prosecuting DUI cases; driver impairment; fluid analysis; and alcohol in the workplace, and more.

Topics covered

- Alcohol and the law
- Biochemistry and physiology of alcohol
- Blood, urine, and other fluid/tissue specimens for alcohol analyses
- Analysis for alcohol in postmortem specimens
- Computer tools for body alcohol evaluation
- Breath as a specimen for analysis for ethanol and other low molecular weigh alcohols

Product Code: 0888 • 536 pages • Casebound • 8.5x11

Oklahoma DUI Defense: The Law & Practice

by Bruce Edge, John Hunsucker and James Nesci

With legislative developments, the introduction of blood alcohol-testing techniques, and an increasingly harsh prosecutorial climate, mounting a successful DUI defense in Oklahoma is more difficult than ever. With our brand new Oklahoma DUI Defense: The Law and Practice, though, you are equipped with a powerful weapon.

This book ensures that you understand the chemical, biological, and technological concepts and issues underlying DUI prosecution and defense, with Oklahoma-specific advice that you couldn't get from any other book.

Many practical tools and applications designed to streamline and simplify the complex DUI defense process are available on a bonus CD-ROM—so you can locate, review and print them out in a matter of seconds. Among this bonus material are DRE and NHSTA student and instructor manuals, and numerous validation studies.

Topics covered

- Advertising
- Client Relations
- DUI and the Oklahoma Motor Vehicle Division
- Pre-trial Investigations
- Pre-trial Motions Practice
- Plea Offers and Agreements
- DUI Trial Procedures
- DUI Investigations, Driving & Field Sobriety Testing
- Drug Recognition Evaluation
- Chemical Testing
- Blood Alcohol Calculations
- Expert Witnesses
- Oklahoma Case Law

Product Code: 4292 • 308 pages • Casebound • 8.5x11

Arizona DUI Defense: The Law & Practice

by James Nesci

For even the most seasoned Arizona Attorney, defending DUI cases has always presented special challenges. Today, due to legislative developments, the introduction of blood alcohol-testing technologies, and an increasingly harsh prosecutorial climate, mounting a successful defense is more difficult than ever. That's why Arizona attorneys will come to rely on Arizona DUI Defense: The Law and Practice.

Written by James Nesci, Board Certified by the National College for DUI Defense and Arizona DUI law expert, Arizona DUI Defense: The Law and Practice ensures that you understand the chemical, biological and technological concepts and issues underlying DUI prosecution and defense in the State of Arizona. You may rely on James Nesci for up-to-date information on key areas.

Included on a bonus CD-ROM are many practical tools and applications designed to streamline and simplify the complex DUI defense process.

Topics covered

- Types of DUI
- Role of the Motor Vehicle Division
- Pre-trial investigation
- DUI investigations
- Driving behavior
- Field sobriety testing
- Drug Recognition
- Chemical testing for alcohol and drugs
- Blood alcohol calculations
- Use of expert witnesses
- DUI jury trial information
- Client relations
- Ethics and advertising
- Arizona Rules of Evidence
- Notices of proposed rulemaking

Product Code: 4144 • 320 pages • Casebound • 8.5x11

Blood Alcohol Concentration Calculator

by Steve Weintraub

This slide calculator contains up-to-date data for estimating BAC, including:

- The Blood Alcohol Concentration (BAC) of men and women from 85–300 lbs. after drinking known amounts of alcoholic beverages,
- The number of specific mixed drinks, beers, wines, and/or distilled spirits consumed from a known BAC level,
- The BAC for each hour (from 0–19) after consumption, and the number of hours required for BAC to fall to a level of choice.

The calculator also compares BAC from the number of drinks of all types of alcoholic beverages.

Product Code: 0618 • Slide calculator

Drugs of Abuse Calculator

by Steve Weintraub

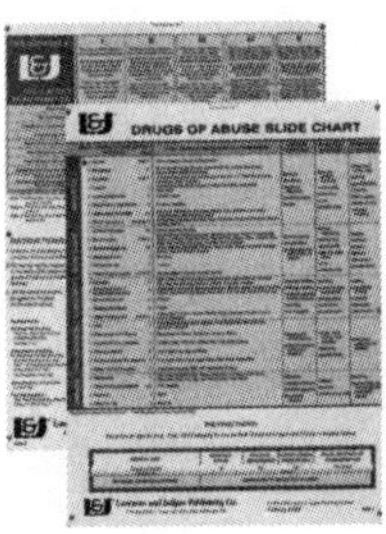

This calculator is loaded with information on drugs of abuse. Now one simple tool will give you trafficking penalties, street names, CSA Regulatory Requirements, and more. All the information contained in volumes of books and regulations right at your fingertips. Side one lists the trade and street names of narcotics, depressants, stimulants, hallucinogens, and cannabis, along with the effects, withdrawal symptoms, and overdose effects.

Also included are the medical use and physical appearance of the drug, methods of administration, detection time in urine, and physical or psychological dependence. Side two provides the CSA Regulatory Requirements and Federal Trafficking Penalties Guide. All information compiled from DEA, CSA, and National Institute on Drug Abuse Data.

Product Code: 0622 • Slide calculator

PremierBAC: Blood Alcohol Concentration Software

by David N. Dresser

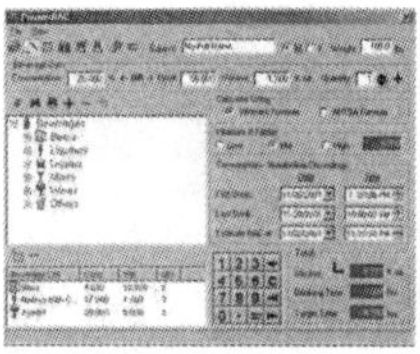

This software can calculate a person's peak blood alcohol concentration, a person's BAC after a specified time after the last drink. It gives you the option of using the two industry-standard equations for better accuracy.

Here is how it works. You provide the person's sex and weight, and either type in the fluid ounces and proof of the drinks, or select common drinks like brand-name beers or daiquiris from a list. The list of common beverages includes their serving size and proof so you don't have to know either of those things! You can request a BAC from a specific time since last drink, as well. Next, you choose from the two standard equations for calculating BAC: the Widmark or the NHSTA equation. You can easily perform both equations for the same person to verify accuracy. After the necessary information is entered, you will see the person's peak BAC and BAC after your specified time period. If you prefer to use the equations without the wizard to help you calculate the amount of alcohol in various drinks, you can do that too! This program is very versatile and contains very useful help screens to guide you on your way.

Note: CD-ROM is compatible with Windows 95, ME, NT and XP only. It is NOT compatible with Windows Vista. It performs best with a minimum of 32MB RAM.

Product Code: 5606 • Software

Download our catalog and view our entire product line at:

online

www.lawyersandjudges.com

Lawyers & Judges Publishing Company, Inc.

P.O. Box 30040 • Tucson, AZ 85751

phone 800.209.7109 • **fax** 800.330.8795

email sales@lawyersandjudges.com